25570

South Knox Middle/High School

W9-BEL-079

54040
Chemical and Biological Weapons:
Anthrax and Sarin

Gregory Payan
AR B.L.: 6.7
Points: 1.0   MG

358
LEV

#25570

PROPERTY OF
SOUTH KNOX SCHOOLS

CHEMICAL & BIOLOGICAL WEAPONS IN OUR TIMES

HERBERT M. LEVINE

FRANKLIN WATTS
A Division of Grolier Publishing
New York • London • Toronto • Sydney
Danbury, Connecticut

PROPERTY OF
SO   KNOX SCHOOLS

DEDICATION

FOR NAEEM AND SALIMA RATHORE

ACKNOWLEDGMENTS

I am grateful for the help of editors at Franklin Watts, particularly Mark Friedman, Executive Editor, for his support, and Martha Cushman, editor, for her editorial attention. Dr. Michael Moodie, President, and Jonathan Ban, Research Associate, of the Chemical and Biological Arms Control Institute, made insightful and helpful recommendations. I also wish to thank Richard B. Beal, Jr., for his comments on the manuscript.

—Herbert M. Levine

Cover and interior design by Molly Heron
Photographs©: AP/Wide World Photos: 16, 27, 103, 104; Corbis-Bettmann: 58 (AFP), 38 (Reuters), 51, 57 (UPI), 20, 87; Custom Medical Stock Photo: 32 (B.S.I.P.); Liaison Agency, Inc.: 54 (ABC Ajansi), 75 (Stephen Ferry), 45, 46 (Hulton Getty), 74 (Erik Lesser), 39 (Edwin Remsberg), 19 (Anthony Suau); Omni-Photo Communications: 24 (Grace Davies); Photo Researchers: 26 (Biophoto Associates); Sygma: 9 (Epix), cover (J. P. Laffont), 63, 67 (J. Langevin), 7 (Nikkan Sports), 61 (J. Pavlovsky), 6 (Asahi Shimbun) 21, 36.

Visit Franklin Watts on the Internet at:
http://publishing.grolier.com

Library of Congress Cataloging-In-Publication Data

Levine, Herbert M.
Chemical and biological weapons in our times / Herbert M. Levine.
    p. cm.
Includes bibliographical references and index.
Summary: Examines the history and development of chemical and biological weapons and discusses their proliferation, association with terrorism, and efforts to control their use.
ISBN 0-531-11852-5
1. Chemical warfare—Juvenile literature. 2. Chemical agents (Munitions)—Juvenile literature. 3. Biological warfare—Juvenile literature. 4. Biological weapons—Juvenile literature. [1. Chemical warfare. 2. Biological warfare] I. Title.

UG447 .L447 2000
358'.34—dc21   99-049982

© 2000 Franklin Watts, a Division of Grolier Publishing Company
All rights reserved. Published simultaneously in Canada.
Printed in the United States of America.

GROLIER
PUBLISHING   2 3 4 5 6 7 8 9 10 R 09 08 07 06 05 04 03 02 01

CONTENTS

TERROR IN THE SUBWAY: ATTACK WITH A CHEMICAL WEAPON

O N THE MORNING of March 20, 1995, in Tokyo, many people were going to work. Five men boarded three separate subway trains in different parts of the city and sat down among the passengers. Each train would pass through Kasumigaseki, the station near many of Tokyo's government offices.

The men, who were members of a small group called Aum Shinrikyo (Supreme Truth), carried plastic bags that looked like lunch bags. Newspapers covered the bags. The men also had umbrellas with sharp points. The men put the bags on the floor of the subway cars. A few stops before Kasumigaseki, the men pushed down the umbrellas, punching holes in the bags. They left the bags in the subway cars and then quickly exited the subways and train stations.

Within minutes, oily liquid seeped through the bags. As the trains moved from station to station, a sickening smell floated through the air. People gagged and gasped for breath. They moved away as the smell became more and more offensive, and then they began to panic. When the trains reached a station, they fled from the cars. Some people suddenly felt dizzy, and some collapsed on station platforms. Others felt nauseous and began to have vision problems—some of them couldn't see at all. Many people coughed, vomited, or felt as if they were choking. Those who had enough strength staggered out of the station in search of fresh air.

An old man who had been sitting next to a leaking package in one of the subway cars became motionless and soon died. In one of the trains, an assistant station manager used a mop in an attempt to clean up the liquid on the floor of the car, and another subway worker helped him. Both soon fell ill and died. The same poisonous liquid that had made the passengers sick also affected the police and subway employees who tried to help people. Emergency workers wearing gas masks and special clothing that protected them against poisonous chemicals arrived on the scene. They moved the injured victims to the street.

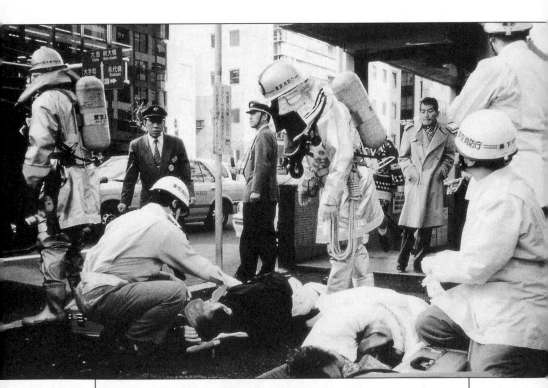

Emergency workers in Tokyo treat some victims of the 1995 Aum Shinrikyo sarin attack on the streets outside the subway stations.

The nature of the attack created confusion among emergency workers—in part, because the smell of gas had been reported at 15 stations. The streets in downtown Tokyo, a large city, were packed with traffic. Emergency vehicles had trouble reaching their destinations. Emergency workers set up tents outside the subway stations in the middle of the chaos. The streets looked like a battlefield, except that many of the wounded were wearing business clothes rather than military uniforms. Injured people lay on the ground in pain. Some had bubbles coming from their mouths, and others had blood flowing from their noses. Doctors and nurses helped them as best they could.

Ambulance after ambulance rushed to the subway stations and carried the victims to more than 100 hospitals. The large number of casualties crowded the hospitals, with injured people sprawled on chairs and floors of emergency rooms. In all, the disaster killed 12 people and injured more than 5,000. Most people recovered, but some were left with serious, permanent

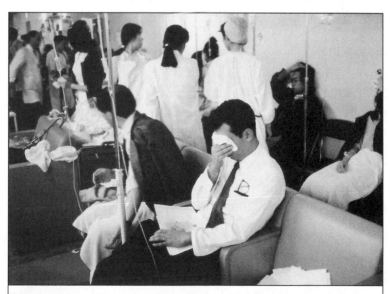

Some victims of the Aum Shinrikyo sarin attack, which occurred in a Tokyo subway one morning in 1995, needed hospital treatment.

problems, such as blindness. The men who released the liquid in the subways were not among the casualties, because they had earlier taken an *antidote*—a remedy that counteracts the effects of a poison.

The Tokyo police took three hours to determine that *sarin*, a poisonous nerve agent, caused the disaster (see Chapter 1). Sarin is 500 times more poisonous than cyanide, the gas used in some states to kill convicted murderers. Sarin is so poisonous that half of one-thousandth of a gram—smaller than a speck of salt and invisible to the naked eye—is enough to kill an average-sized adult.

The disaster in Tokyo's subways could have been even worse for three reasons. First, the trains were not as crowded as they usually were on Monday mornings, because the attack took place the day before a national holiday when many people did not go to work. Second, the sarin was in the form of a liquid rather than a gas. Had it been in the form of a gas, thousands of people might have died. Third, because the people who prepared this batch of sarin were in a hurry, there were impurities in it, weakening it considerably. A pure nerve agent would have killed thousands of people within minutes, because treatment for exposure to nerve gas must begin within one or two minutes or it is useless.

The Japanese people wondered who would commit such a horrible act. Nobody took responsibility for the crime. Acts of reckless killing and maiming were uncommon in Japan, a country with one of the lowest violent crime rates in the world. The Japanese police had their suspicions, however. They had been receiving information about the criminal activities of Aum Shinrikyo, a religious group, including reports about the manufacture of sarin and even about murder. The police had been investigating the organization but hesitated to move against it for fear that they would be accused of religious persecution.

Within days of the subway attack, the police raided 30 offices of Aum Shinrikyo. They discovered two tons of chemicals, some of which could be used in the manufacture of sarin. They also found gas masks. The police concluded that Aum was responsible for the sarin attack, but Shoko Asahara, Aum's leader, denied this charge. He accused the Japanese government of committing the crime in order to turn Japanese public opinion against his religious organization.

Once law-enforcement officials and members of the press found out about Aum Shinrikyo, people in Japan and around the world soon learned more about the group. Aum beliefs are based on Buddhist and Hindu teachings, but the activities of

Shoko Asahara was the leader of the religious group Aum Shinrikyo when some of its members carried out the 1995 sarin attack in the Tokyo subways.

the group are not typical of people who follow Buddhism and Hinduism. Asahara preached that Armageddon—the final battle between good and evil that, according to a biblical prophecy, will occur at the end of the world—was fast approaching in Japan. Asahara said it would occur between 1996 and 1998. According to Aum beliefs, salvation would only come at the end of Armageddon to those who adopt the Aum faith. It would come for those Aum members who had reached a higher state of thinking than anyone else through the teachings of the "Supreme Master"—Asahara.

Aum Shinrikyo claimed to have 10,000 to 30,000 followers worldwide. It required that members turn over their entire income to the organization. Aum officials forced members who were critical of the group to remain in it. According to the police, Aum leaders punished some of these people by putting them in a kind of prison. They even ordered the murder of some members who had turned against the group as well as some critics who did not belong to it. The murderers disposed of some of the bodies by secretly burying them at Aum headquarters.

People in the outside world could not understand why members of Aum Shinrikyo launched the chemical attack. But the group had a definite purpose. It had been warned about possible trouble with the police and wanted to avoid a raid. Aum hoped that by killing and injuring thousands of people, it could prevent government agencies, particularly the police, from taking action against it. Aum also wanted to show that it was ready to fight a war against the government and the police.

After the sarin attack, law-enforcement authorities learned that beginning in 1987, Aum Shinrikyo purchased materials in the United States to produce chemical and biological weapons. Then the group recruited scientists and technicians in Japan and other countries such as Russia to learn how to produce these weapons. While Aum was gathering essential materials and information, it pretended to engage in lawful commercial operations.

Aum Shinrikyo began to use some of the products it had created in ways that had nothing to do with normal business dealings. In 1993, Aum tried to infect some people in Tokyo with a disease called *anthrax,* which infects animals and can be transmitted to human beings. Fortunately, this attempt failed. Then, in 1994, Aum members sprayed sarin over an apartment complex in Matsumoro, Japan, in an attempt to kill the judges who were part of a noncriminal trial in which Aum was a participant. Aum's agents did not succeed in killing the judges, although the sarin made them ill. But seven people who lived in the apartment complex died, and more than 500 were injured. Aum had engaged in other biological and chemical attacks too.

When the police raided the facilities of Aum Shinrikyo after the sarin attack in Tokyo, they discovered a large supply of anthrax and *botulinum toxin,* a deadly substance (see Chapter 1). Investigators also learned that Aum planned to attack New York City and Washington, D.C. In the past, Aum had tested sarin on sheep in Australia and had built factories where chemical, biological, and *conventional weapons*—weapons other than chemical, biological, and nuclear weapons, such as guns and tanks—could be manufactured. Aum could afford to engage in these activities because it was a wealthy organization, with property and other possessions worth more than $1 billion.

The Tokyo subway assault was the first case in which a private group successfully attacked civilians with chemical weapons on a large scale. People were horrified. Government officials who were responsible for the security of nations and communities wondered about the future. If a little-known, relatively small group could secretly produce chemical weapons that could kill or injure thousands of people in a civilized country like Japan, then other groups could do this too. Would the people of any community ever be safe from similar attacks— or attacks that were even worse?.

What happened in Tokyo could occur in any city. In the United States, government officials recognized the danger. They knew that sarin is not the only dangerous chemical weapon that could cause large numbers of casualties. Some chemical agents are hundreds of times deadlier than sarin. The officials understood that biological weapons, such as anthrax, could be just as dangerous, and probably even more deadly, than chemical weapons. Under certain conditions, biological weapons could kill hundreds of thousands, perhaps millions, of people. The populations of entire cities were at risk.

The sarin attack on the Tokyo subways shows that an independent, private group can obtain and use chemical weapons. Even people who work alone could cause many injuries or deaths using chemical or biological weapons. Or governments could be behind attacks using these weapons.

These attacks could come "out of the blue" or in the course of armed conflict with another country. Civilians or military forces could be the targets. The United States has many enemies who have sponsored acts of violence against American targets overseas. Many officials began to believe that it is not a matter of "if" but rather "when" attacks with chemical and biological weapons will occur against Americans—in the United States or other countries.

The targets could be civilians, or even ethnic groups, or groups that seek independence from a country. Or they could be soldiers. For example, during the Iran-Iraq War, Iraq used chemical weapons against Iran. U.S. leaders feared an Iraqi chemical attack against the armed forces of the United States and its allies in the Persian Gulf War of 1991.

But is anyone likely to succeed in causing terrible damage that will claim the lives of millions of people and contaminate the land? What is the United States doing to prevent such an attack from happening or to limit the damage that would result? What are other countries doing about possible attacks? These questions must be answered if we are to understand the dangers of chemical and biological weapons.

CHAPTER 1

WEAPONS OF HORROR

Over time, people have learned to make products that are both creative and destructive. When people learned how to work with metal and mold it in certain ways, they built plows that could help raise crops to feed the hungry. But that same metal could be turned into swords to kill people. In recent years, scientists have developed chemical compounds to make useful commercial products, such as insecticides and ballpoint pens. Some of these same chemicals can be used to make chemical weapons that cause death or long-term injury.

In addition, scientists have developed *vaccines*, or preparations of microorganisms that are given for protection against certain diseases, to save lives. They used biological *cultures*, or populations of microorganisms prepared in nutrient media, to help cure the diseases. But some of these organisms that can be put to good use can also spread disease and kill people.

All weapons cause damage, but what makes many chemical and biological materials so dangerous is the extent of the damage they can produce. They are *weapons of mass destruction* (WMD). Chemical and biological weapons are two of the three kinds of WMD, and nuclear weapons are the third type. (These three kinds of weapons are sometimes known as NBC weapons [nuclear, biological, chemical].)

Like chemical and biological weapons, nuclear weapons can kill hundreds of thousands, if not millions, of people. Some Americans have feared a nuclear attack since 1949, when the Soviet Union tested a nuclear device. But unlike chemical and biological weapons, nuclear weapons are so difficult and expensive to make that relatively few countries have developed them. And international agencies keep track of such items as reactors and nuclear fuels that are needed for the manufacture of these powerful weapons.

In contrast, chemical and biological weapons are relatively easy to make. Many of their components are widely available throughout the world, where they are used for commercial and medical purposes. These substances are inexpensive, although the costs of turning them into weapons can be high.

Still, a chemical or biological weapon costs less to produce than a nuclear weapon does. Because of the relatively low cost, a chemical or biological weapon is sometimes called "the poor man's atomic bomb." In general, it is easier to identify facilities that produce nuclear weapons than to recognize factories used for the production of chemical and biological weapons. It is much more difficult for governments and international organizations to monitor chemical and biological weapons than it is for them to detect nuclear weapons and their components. Some developing nations have acquired chemical and biological weapons because they seem to provide security (see Chapter 4).

In addition to taking the lives of large numbers of people and demolishing buildings, WMD can destroy plants, kill animals, and cause extensive environmental damage. Under certain conditions, conventional weapons can also cause severe destruction, but even in the worst situations, the damage would occur over a longer period of time and require a much larger military operation. Because of the destructive power of chemical and biological weapons, it is important to understand the nature of chemical and biological warfare agents, their effects, and how they are used. It is also important to know what methods of protection are available to military personnel and civilians.

Chemical and Biological Warfare Agents: Similarities and Differences

Chemical warfare is the intentional use of *toxic* (poisonous) substances resulting in death or injury. Chemical weapons differ from conventional weapons in that they rely on chemical effects rather than physical effects, such as blast and heat, to produce damage. Both kinds of weapons contain chemicals, however. *Biological warfare* is the intentional use of microorganisms or *toxins* (poisonous substances made by living organisms or synthetic processes) to produce death or disease in humans, animals, or plants.

Chemical and biological weapons have many similarities, as the following list indicates. Both of these weapons can

- Be produced relatively inexpensively (compared to other weapons)
- Injure and kill people, poison plants and animals, pollute water, and contaminate land
- Harm living things rather than cause physical damage
- Produce effects over large areas
- Be set off in the air and reach targets wherever the air circulates
- Be manufactured in the same facilities used to make commercial products
- Be delivered in a variety of ways, including artillery, multiple rocket launchers, tactical ballistic missiles, strategic ballistic missiles, *cruise missiles* (vehicles carrying a warhead that are guided automatically or by distant human control), manned aircraft, and unmanned flying vehicles. Simple sources, such as boats, trucks, automobiles, or even individuals carrying sprayers, can also *disperse*, or scatter, the agents.

Aerial bombs, such as these from Iraq, which were destroyed by UN inspectors in 1998, can be used to deliver chemical and biological warfare agents.

But chemical and biological weapons have many differences too, as the following list suggests:

- Chemical weapons kill or injure by poisoning, while biological agents kill or injure by causing disease.
- Chemical weapons affect only those who come into contact with them. But some biological weapons may spread beyond the people who are initially affected as a result of *epidemics*—outbreaks of contagious diseases.
- Biological weapons are slightly more difficult to manufacture than chemical weapons because they involve sensitive living organisms.
- Biological agents are less expensive to produce than chemical agents.

- Chemical weapons require much bigger facilities to produce and much more storage space than biological weapons.
- The effects of chemical weapons are generally almost instantaneous, while the effects of biological weapons take time to develop.
- When spread properly under ideal conditions involving weather, population density, quality of construction, and other characteristics, one biological weapon can kill 100 to 1,000 times as many people compared to one chemical weapon of the same weight.

Chemical and Biological Weapons: Usefulness as Weapons

Many military analysts believe that chemical agents are superior to biological agents for use in warfare because chemical weapons are more stable and easier to manufacture. They are usually more predictable in action than biological agents too.

To be used successfully in warfare, chemical or biological weapons must have the following characteristics and methods of delivery:

- The agents must be able to be produced in quantity.
- The amount must be large enough to affect the targeted population.
- The agents must be stored safely so that they do not *corrode*, or wear away gradually, the containers. (Rust is a kind of corrosion.)
- The agents must be able to "survive" until they reach their destination.
- The agents must be dispersed so that all the targeted individuals are affected.

In addition, the people who use biological weapons must know whether the agents cause a contagious disease. Because biological agents need time to take effect, those who use a biological weapon must decide whether the time factor works to their advantage or presents a problem.

Just being able to develop or obtain a chemical or biological warfare agent may be insufficient to turn it into a successful weapon if the conditions for its use are not right. For example, members of Aum Shinrikyo released anthrax over Tokyo in 1993. Although some people complained of illness, the anthrax apparently did not succeed in killing anyone. In 1998, reporters from the *New York Times* conducted an investigation based on court testimony, confessions of Aum members, and interviews with Japanese and American government officials. The reporters concluded that Aum used biological agents in nine attacks, which failed because the germs Aum used were not poisonous enough.

Chemical Weapons: Sometimes Irritating, Often Lethal

In its broadest sense, a chemical weapon may be defined as any chemical that can be used in war. Perhaps a narrower definition is better—a chemical that is highly toxic and is capable of being used primarily to cause harm to people and animals.

Chemical weapons may be classified in different ways. They may be described as persistent or nonpersistent, and lethal or irritant. Persistent agents have effects over a long time after they have been released. Nonpersistent agents dissipate—or separate and vanish—after several minutes. *Lethal agents* are substances that cause death. With some chemical substances, death may come in hours or even days, while with others, it can take minutes. Sometimes, a low dosage of a lethal agent may injure but not kill an individual. *Irritant agents,* sometimes known as *harassing agents*, are substances that affect the senses. Unless they are taken in large doses, they are not lethal.

The major types of irritant agents are *lachrymators, sternutators,* and *orticants.* Lachrymators produce a flow of tears that temporarily blinds people as long as the substance is in the air. For example, tear gas is a lachrymator. Sternutators cause sneezing and coughing and may prevent people from wearing gas masks. Orticants produce an itchy rash or a stinging sensation.

Chemical weapons can also be classified by the effects they produce. *Choking agents,* sometimes called respiratory agents, such as *chlorine, phosgene,* and the related diphosgene, are lethal substances that first appeared as weapons of war in World War I. Choking agents prevent people from breathing by causing

Tear gas can be used for purposes of crowd control, as at this antigovernment protest in South Korea.

American troops in France advance against the enemy in World War I (1918). Most of the soldiers are wearing gas masks. A soldier who seemingly is unable to wear a mask is afflicted by gas and clutches his throat.

inflammation of the lung tissue, which leads to the entry of large quantities of fluids from the bloodstream into the lungs. Victims "drown" from inside when their respiratory system cuts off their oxygen supply. These chemical weapons have an odor that warns people to take defensive measures, such as putting on gas masks and protective clothing. If these protective steps are taken in time, the individuals may avoid death. More modern lethal agents have no odors, and therefore they are more likely to kill people before they are detected. In addition, modern chemical agents are more toxic than those used in World War I.

Blistering agents, or *vesicants,* are toxic substances that cause wounds to the skin and mucous membranes—the tissues that line body cavities such as the mouth and nose. As their name suggests, blistering agents cause blisters within a few

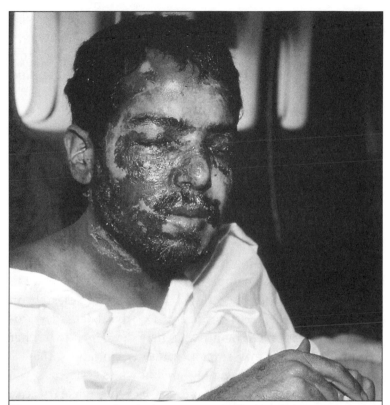

Exposure to some chemical agents may lead to injuries, such as the blisters and burns on the face of this Iranian man who was a victim of chemical warfare. He is receiving treatment in a hospital in Austria.

hours from the time that they come into contact with their target. The results are often fatal. During World War I, Germans introduced the blistering agent *mustard gas* (dichlorethyl sulfide), which smells like mustard or garlic. Mustard gas irritated the eyes and throats of the soldiers and caused blisters to form on their skin. Sometimes it led to blindness, vomiting, and nausea that lasted for months. Death resulted from damage to the respiratory system. In addition, mustard gas contaminated the soil, so it had to be removed before people could walk in areas where it had been used.

Lewisite, another blistering agent whose effects are similar to those of mustard gas, was developed in 1918 in an attempt to produce a highly toxic, nonpersistent, quick-acting compound. It caused severe eye damage within 15 minutes and blistering within eight hours.

Blood agents are substances that are absorbed into the body through inhalation. These substances interfere with the transport of oxygen through the body by damaging body tissues. Blood agents can be lethal within 15 minutes. People may die by *asphyxiation* (suffocation). The principal blood agents are hydrogen cyanide and cyanogen chloride. Most blood agents are derivatives of cyanide compounds.

Nerve agents are lethal substances that disable the enzymes essential to transmitting messages between nerves and muscles. (An enzyme is a complex protein needed by the body to carry out biochemical reactions.) While doing research on insecticides in 1936, German scientist Gerhard Schrader produced tabun. Soon German researchers developed two other nerve gases—sarin and soman. Tabun, sarin, and soman—three highly toxic nerve agents—are known as G-agents.

Because these nerve agents are so toxic, they make effective killing agents. The nerve agents act quickly when they are absorbed through the skin or inhaled. Nerve agents block nerve function and lead to death as a result of paralysis of the respiratory system. G-series gases can cause death in 1 to 10 minutes. (By comparison, phosgene requires 4 to 24 hours to kill.) Nerve agents may be dispersed as a cloud of vapor or as a spray of liquid droplets. Unlike the poisonous gases used in World War I, nerve agents give off little odor, which means that they can cause injury or death before they are even detected. (In the case of the Aum Shinrikyo attack on the Tokyo subways in 1995, impurities in the sarin caused the foul odor.) Nerve agents can cause breathing problems and make people confused. Eventually, nerve agents cause convulsions and death.

V-series nerve agents, such as *VX*, which scientists developed during the 1950s, are even more powerful than G-agents.

Small doses of V-agents can penetrate skin and contaminate the ground, plants, and equipment. If absorbed through the skin, they are 2,000 times more toxic than mustard gas. Experts calculate that under the proper conditions, 500 tons of VX is enough to cover an area of 1,250 square miles (about 3,200 square kilometers). They believe that such a quantity is three times the poison needed to contaminate 10 typical military airfields and areas for assembling 100 infantry battalions. It could seriously threaten half a dozen cities as well.

Hundreds of thousands of unprotected civilians in cities could be killed in this way. But V-agents must be manufactured, stored, and delivered in certain ways, or they may not have the desired effect.

In World War I, chlorine and phosgene were the principal chemical agents used in warfare. Both of these gases are lung irritants that can kill. Today, chemical weapons are primarily either liquids or solids that can be given off in the form of powders, smoke formations, or *aerosols*—suspensions of small, fine particles in either a solid, liquid, or gas in which they are sometimes dispersed. (Fog and smoke are aerosols.)

Producing Chemical Weapons: Is It Difficult?

People who want to *synthesize* chemical weapons, or make them by combining other substances, may find that it is relatively simple to manufacture some of these harmful agents. Production involves many processes that are adapted from standard engineering principles. Some agents, such as mustard gas, are easy to produce. Information about building a chemical weapon is familiar to many chemists, and the literature about chemical weapons is easily accessible.

Manufacture does not require factories that make only military products. Chemical agents can be produced in factories that make commercial products because both can use the same *precursors* (substances from which other products are formed) and equipment. Any country with a petrochemical—chemical made from petroleum or natural gas, such as plastic—or fertilizer industry can make chemical weapons. It takes only a short time (weeks or months) to turn a commercial plant that makes fertilizer into a military plant that makes nerve agents.

A chemical agent may have two uses—a commercial use and a weapons-related use. Such an agent is known as a *dual-purpose chemical.* For example, the chemical thiodiglycol has two purposes. Not only is it used as a solvent in making ink for ballpoint pens, lubricant additives, plastics, and photographic developing solutions, but it is also an important ingredient in

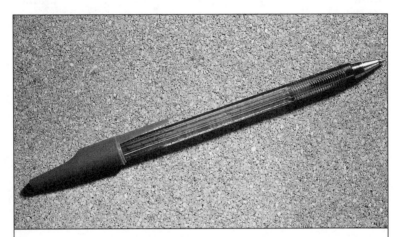

Thiodiglycol, a solvent used to make ink for ballpoint pens, is also an ingredient in mustard gas.

mustard gas. Another dual-purpose substance, a precursor of fluoride toothpaste, can be used in the development of a chemical weapon. During World War I, alcohol, bleaching powder, and sodium sulfite were used to produce thousands of tons of mustard gas.

Some of the same equipment used in the manufacture of chemical weapons is also used in the commercial chemical industry. The same reactor vessels, distillation columns, heat exchangers, pumps and valves, and filters are employed.

There are similarities in the manufacture of nerve gases and insecticides. Conversion from a commercial plant to a military plant that manufactures nerve agents might take only weeks or months. One expert has stated that any country that can produce pesticides probably has the technology and expertise to manufacture nerve agents.

But the manufacture of chemical weapons agents requires large sites—both to produce the poisonous substances and to store them once they have been made. The chemical plants give off waste gases that can be detected and monitored.

Safety considerations require that chemical weapons be manufactured so that they can be transported under various weather conditions. For example, chemical weapons must be able to withstand temperature changes, so that they don't weaken. Some agents are composed of compounds that are highly corrosive so they must be stored in containers that resist corrosion. Unfortunately, safety is not as important in some countries as it is in the United States.

To avoid risks to the personnel who manufacture and transport chemical weapons, researchers developed binary technology. *Binary weapons* involve using separate containers to isolate two substances that are dangerous when combined. Only when the weapon, such as a bomb, *projectile* (self-propelling missile), or grenade, is heading for its target do the substances in the two containers mix together and combine to form a deadly chemical weapon. This procedure makes them safe to transport.

Biological Weapons: Bacteria, Viruses, and More

Some biological agents may kill people, animals, or plants, while others cause severe injury. Microorganisms that cause disease may be classified into several groups—*bacteria*, including the *rickettsiae; viruses*; and *fungi*. Toxins are also biological weapons.

Bacteria are microscopic, single-cell organisms that carry out a wide range of biochemical processes. They may have beneficial effects, such as enriching the soil. Bacteria, however, may cause disease either by invading body tissues or by producing toxins that have a harmful effect. When bacteria or viruses invade the human body, they may lead to infection. Bacteria cause strep throat and diseases such as dysentery, undulant fever, cholera, diphtheria, Lyme disease, salmonella, pulmonary tuberculosis, and bubonic plague.

The rickettsiae are a group of bacteria that must be grown in living tissue. Diseases caused by rickettsiae include Q fever, typhus, and Rocky Mountain spotted fever.

Anthrax is an example of a biological weapon. Anthrax, an infectious disease of animals that is caused by a bacterium, can be transmitted from animals to humans. Death results from pneumonia (lung disease), infections, and organ failure. The bacterium that causes anthrax is *Bacillus anthracis*. Like some

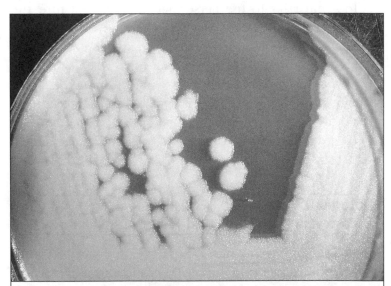

Some bacteria, such as *Bacillus anthracis*, which causes the deadly disease known as anthrax, can be used as biological weapons. The bacteria can be cultured on a petri dish.

other bacteria, this organism forms *spores*—protective cells with a hard coating that allows bacteria to exist in an inactive state for years. If the spores reach an environment that is warm and moist, such as the lungs, they become active. Inhaling a few thousand anthrax spores—less than it takes to cover a pinhead—can be deadly unless the infected person is quickly treated with antibiotics.

Anthrax can cause disease and contaminate soil for years. In 1943, Great Britain conducted a test that involved the release of anthrax on the island of Gruinard, off the northwest coast of Scotland. The purpose of the test was to estimate how much

Gruinard Island off the coast of Scotland was sealed off from the public for almost a half century in an effort to decontaminate the land. The island had been used for field trials in 1943 to assess the use of anthrax spores as a potential biological weapon.

anthrax would be required for attacks on cities. Despite many efforts to clean up the site after the test, the island was not considered safe for unprotected visitors until the 1990s. According to a Central Intelligence Agency (CIA) publication, one gram of anthrax—which weighs about as much as a paper clip—could kill more than one-third of the U.S. population under ideal conditions.

Viruses—organisms that are 100 times smaller than bacteria—consist of genetic material surrounded by a protective coat. After they invade cells, they multiply and cause disease. Some viral diseases are influenza, acquired immunodeficiency syndrome (AIDS), chickenpox, mumps, measles, yellow fever, dengue fever, smallpox, hepatitis, Ebola, and Venezuelan equine encephalitis. The Ebola virus, which was unknown until recently, has no known cure and usually kills within days of infection. Bacteria and viruses are living organisms that reproduce and multiply, so they are known as "replicating" agents.

Fungi are organisms that are responsible for the decay and decomposition of organic matter. Although they do not generally cause disease in people, they destroy staple crops such as wheat and rice, which many people depend on for food. In this way, they produce hunger and lead to economic problems.

Toxins can also cause disease. These poisonous substances, which are produced by living organisms or synthetic processes, may also harm humans and other animals. (Because they are chemical compounds, toxins are sometimes described as chemical, not biological, weapons. Unlike biological agents, toxins cannot reproduce and multiply.)

Botulinum toxin, which is produced by the bacterium *Clostridium botulinum*, is among the world's most toxic substances. One kind of botulinum toxin is 10,000 times more poisonous than the venom from a cobra, a poisonous snake. Food that contains botulinum toxin results in the disease called *botulism*, which leads to problems with vision, speech, and swallowing and causes paralysis of the respiratory muscles, resulting in suffocation. Botulinum toxin acts relatively quickly, and death occurs in one to three days in 80 percent of the people who are affected. *Ricin,* which is made from castor beans, is another deadly toxin. Death results from inhaling a very small amount, about 10 micrograms (ten-millionths of a gram).

Different biological agents have different effects. Some, such as anthrax, are usually lethal, while others, such as the Venezuelan equine encephalitis virus, weaken people by causing nausea, vomiting, sore throat, and diarrhea. Some biological agents lose their strength by heat, sunlight, and drying. Others last for long periods of time. Most biological agents are infectious, which means that they affect people who are directly exposed to them. But some biological agents, such as plague bacteria, are highly contagious—they affect people by direct or indirect contact. In the fourteenth century, the Black Death, as the bubonic plague was called, killed as many as 20 to 30 million people in Europe alone—up to one-third of the population—as well as an estimated 13 million people in China.

The presence of biological agents is difficult to detect right away. So hundreds of thousands of people may be exposed before they know it. They can't see or taste the agents, and the aerosol clouds are invisible.

Once released, it is difficult to control biological weapons. Many factors come into play, including meteorological (relating to the atmosphere, especially weather) conditions, the topography (physical features of the land), and the way diseases spread outside of their place of origin. Effectiveness depends on the amount of material that reaches the lungs and remains in the respiratory tract. Wind speed and direction as well as other meteorological factors determine whether an aerosol effectively reaches its target. Environmental factors, such as light and temperature, may also weaken the effectiveness of biological agents.

The actual use of biological weapons in an attack creates other problems. When an organism is placed in a projectile such as a bomb, it is difficult to keep it alive. A biological agent

PROPERTY OF
SOUTHKNOX SCHOOL

or a chemical weapon may be destroyed in the explosion of an artillery shell. Some analysts believe that spraying from aircraft is the only practical and effective means of delivering biological weapons in good condition.

Aerosol sprayers can be no more complicated than the kinds of sprayers sold in agricultural supply houses. The sprayers may disperse the agents from a plane, car, boat, or other source. The spray may be carried over great distances and affect large populations as it is moved along by wind. Biological agents could be dispersed in other ways than by aerosol sprays. For example, they can be put in food or water.

According to one expert, a major attack with anthrax spores over a wide area would require the use of a crop duster with custom-built nozzles. The crop duster is needed to produce a high-concentration aerosol cloud containing particles of anthrax ranging from one to five microns (one- to five-millionths of a meter) in size. That's much less than one-thousandth of an inch! Smaller particles would not remain suspended for long in human lungs, and larger particles would not remain hanging for long in the air. To produce casualties on a large scale, the anthrax would have to be processed into a fine powder, which would require the use of complex and costly equipment. If the anthrax is used in liquid form, its ability to cause mass casualties is reduced.

With many living biological weapons, though, the initial number of organisms may increase rapidly. Biological agents can easily multiply within a short period of time. For example, bacteria can divide every 20 minutes. In 10 hours, one cell can become 1 billion organisms. In days, the bacteria would make a powerful weapon. Experts say that as little as 11 pounds (5 kilograms) of plague bacterial paste could have a devastating military impact on 247 acres (100 hectares), about the same area as 25 city blocks, and could spread disease over wide areas.

In recent years, research developments have produced new possibilities for biological weapons. *Genetic engineering,* or manipulating genetic material (DNA) of cells, has allowed development of new crop plants and increased food production. The technique produces recombinant DNA, which transports selected genes from one species to another. Advances in genetic engineering could allow scientists to create "supergerms" for which there is no known defense. Terrorists and governments may have unique, highly lethal substances at their disposal.

Some experts believe that proposed scenarios for the development and use of such "supergerms" are exaggerated and unlikely to become a reality. For example, they doubt that new genetic engineering techniques will produce *pathogens* that can be effective biological weapons. Pathogens are agents that cause disease. Scientists believe that some stories about "supergerms" that appear in the popular press are unrealistic. These stories suggest that secret attacks could produce diseases in everyone except the few attackers who possess an antidote for the disease or a vaccine against it. The experts doubt that such a dramatic situation will ever occur, because the development, production, storage, and use of these agents involve complicated processes.

Producing Biological Weapons: Can It Be Done Easily?

The information needed to manufacture biological weapons is as widely known as the information needed to make chemical weapons. The published literature on this subject is extensive and easily accessible. Any country with even a modest, relatively small-scale, *pharmaceutical* industry could produce biological warfare agents easily and cheaply as an outgrowth of the manufacture and sale of drugs. Any country with facilities for medical research or industries that rely on *fermentation*—a chemical reaction that splits complex organic compounds into relatively simple substances—can also make biological weapons. Biological agents can be produced using flasks or fermenters, such as those used in making beer.

Most of the equipment needed to manufacture pathogens and toxins may be purchased in the open market throughout the world. Production of biological agents may involve dual-use equipment, such as computer-controlled fermenters, centrifugal separators, freeze-dryers, and spray-dryers, that can be used for commercial and military purposes. Many commercial firms manufacture such equipment.

Strains of viruses and bacteria can be ordered through the mail from laboratory-supply houses and are available in medical laboratories and hospitals. (In the 1990s, though, the federal government imposed regulations concerning access to agents that are potentially hazardous to public health and safety.) Pathogens such as the bacterium that causes bubonic plague can even be cultivated in living animals, including rats and horses. Some pathogens can be obtained from secretions or tissues of sick or dead animals or people.

Dual-use equipment such as this fermenter can be used to make biological agents.

Some advances in medical science also have led to another source for some components of biological weapons. Some highly toxic materials, such as ricin, as well as the botulinum and diphtheria toxins, were long thought to have no practical use. Now they are used or being considered for use for medical purposes. Every year, about one million people in the United States and Europe receive botulinum toxin injections as treatment for a variety of diseases. Individuals who wanted to make biological weapons could obtain these deadly toxins and the research that relates to them without attracting the attention of most intelligence sources.

*   *   *

Although chemical and biological agents are available in large amounts, it is difficult to turn them into effective weapons because of the technical problems involved. It is also difficult to actually commit an attack with chemical or biological weapons before law-enforcement agencies find out about the planned attack and take steps to prevent it.

CHAPTER 2

GUARDING AGAINST THE EFFECTS OF ATTACK

To deal with a problem effectively, you need to understand it. In matters of personal safety, sensible people take steps to avoid danger. If the danger becomes a reality, however, they respond to it intelligently. Strong locks and an alarm system may keep a robber away from your home and offer some protection. But what if someone actually breaks in? The police may respond quickly to an intruder who overcomes protective devices. Dealing with a chemical and biological weapons attack requires the same attention to protection and response to these agents as does attention to personal safety.

As people learned after the sarin attack in the Tokyo subways, protecting oneself against a major chemical or biological weapons attack depends on many factors, including the kind of agent used and how effectively it is dispersed. Many people might die before they even know that they are in danger. Many medical and emergency personnel would be killed or injured, and so they could not help care for people who were victims of the attack. In many situations, it would be too late to provide the vaccines and other medications needed to cure or treat any illnesses the agents caused. There might not be enough medical facilities, drugs, or health-care workers available to cope with the huge number of casualties.

Protective Measures: What People Can Do

Although chemical and biological weapons can cause a tremendous number of casualties, not all attacks result in disaster, sometimes for technical reasons (see Chapters 1 and 5). Also, individuals can take steps to protect themselves. Military personnel, rather than civilians, are better-suited to take some of these protective measures, however, because these actions may require preparations and an understanding of safety procedures that are more readily adopted by trained military personnel.

Protection is important in saving lives. It involves many factors—some as simple as wearing gas masks and special suits. A gas mask may be the most effective protection against a biological weapon. *Collective protection*—the establishment of areas that are free from harmful chemical and biological agents—allows essential emergency workers, such as doctors and nurses, to move about easily and perform their duties. Decontaminating agents that clean up areas is another method of protection. It is important to make sure that medical personnel, facilities, and supplies are readily available for use in treating people who are injured by chemical or biological agents. Lives can be saved and fears are lessened if governments are prepared for such attacks.

If a government suspects that potential enemies are likely to use a particular chemical or biological weapon, it can set up programs that would offer some protection, such as vaccination. The possibility of germ warfare occurring somewhere in the world is real. Because U.S. forces may be in danger from an anthrax attack, Secretary of Defense William Cohen announced in December 1997 that all U.S. military personnel would be inoculated against anthrax. On May 18, 1998, he approved a plan to vaccinate all U.S. armed forces against anthrax, including new recruits, by the year 2003. This is the first time that American troops are receiving routine inoculations against a germ warfare agent.

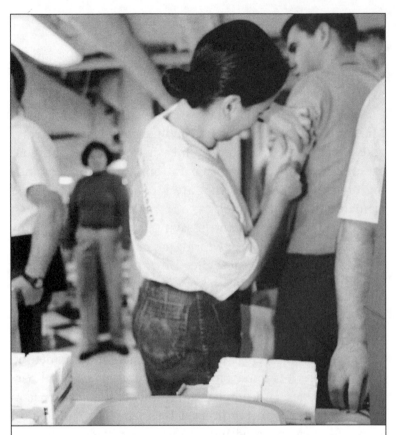

U.S. military personnel are being inoculated against anthrax because they could be exposed to this deadly biological warfare agent.

By February 2000, however, 351 military personnel had refused to take the anthrax vaccine despite threat of military court trials. The Department of Defense rejected the recomendations of some members of Congress who wanted to make the vaccination program voluntary. The department insisted that despite some reports of flulike symptoms and other reactions, the vaccine was safe.

Anthrax vaccination is complicated. It requires multiple doses over several months and booster shots every year. Government officials have estimated that up to 2.4 million members of the armed forces would receive vaccinations. The U.S. Defense Department has calculated that the cost for vaccination against anthrax for the armed forces would be $130 million. No effort is being made to inoculate the entire U.S. population against anthrax because of the high cost and the likelihood of resistance to the idea.

The U.S. Defense Department considers anthrax to be the top choice in biological weapons for germ warfare for the following reasons:

- Anthrax is almost always deadly if not treated early.
- A basic knowledge of biology is sufficient to produce large quantities of spores.
- Spores can be stored for decades without losing their effectiveness.
- Spores can be spread in the air by missiles, rockets, artillery, aerosol bombs, and sprayers.

Like other biological agents, anthrax has no smell and no taste. When released by aerosol spray, it produces no cloud or color. Until the symptoms of anthrax appear, people do not even know they have been exposed to the disease. And for people who have not been vaccinated against the disease, there is no effective treatment.

But at least there is an effective vaccine against anthrax. The U.S. military has a big problem—it does not have vaccinations for some of the other biological agents that may threaten its forces. In 1998, officials listed more than a dozen pathogens or toxins that posed risks to U.S. troops. At the time of the report, the Food and Drug Administration (FDA)—the agency that evaluates drugs—had not approved any antidotes for these agents.

Because some biological and chemical weapons can be set off without attracting the immediate attention created by a conventional bomb, they might well produce harmful effects before people even know they are in danger. Early warning and

An Israeli family wears gas masks as protection against the possible use of chemical weapons by Iraq during the Persian Gulf War.

detection of a chemical or biological weapons attack are essential for protection.

Early detection might allow soldiers and civilians to put on gas masks. Masks that protect people only against biological weapons are available, and these masks are less costly than masks used for protection against chemical weapons. Remaining indoors would help too. So would staying in rooms that are sealed with tape or supplied with filtered air. If there is an advance warning of an attack with biological weapons, it would help to drink boiled water and cook food well. These precautions would provide protection against biological agents that attack the digestive system.

Early warning would also allow people to have antidotes and other medical supplies on hand in case of attack. But chemical and biological warfare agents are often difficult to detect. Although improvements have been made in reducing the amount of time needed to identify these agents, detection takes time. State and local health departments are using state-of-the-art methods to identify strains of infectious agents. The U.S. Department of Defense has stepped up research on warning sensors that could detect and identify agents. Knowledge of the amount of the agent is important too. If the concentrations of the agent are large enough, even people who are vaccinated against a dangerous biological agent may not be protected.

In the most sophisticated germ detectors, air samples are placed in wet solutions—a process that takes at least 45 minutes—to analyze airborne agents. An electronic system would

This poison gas detector could be used to tell people of an attack with a chemical warfare agent so they could take protective steps, such as wearing gas masks.

speed up that process, but, according to defense specialists, it has not been perfected. Detection and identification of biological agents remain a high priority of U.S. defense efforts.

Emergency Responsiveness

Once the chemical or biological weapon has been dispersed, then emergency personnel and others may attempt to decontaminate the affected area. Soap, water, and diluted chlorine bleach are used to clean up biological agents.

Effective measures to improve coordination in the operations of government agencies that provide emergency care can also reduce casualties. The United States has begun to take steps to improve the quality of emergency care in case of attack by chemical or biological weapons. The Defense Against Weapons of Mass Destruction Act of 1996 calls for a program to provide federal resources, training, and technical assistance to the federal, state, and local emergency management personnel who would respond to an incident such as the one on the Tokyo subways. Congress has set aside funds to provide training for local officials in 120 cities. The training involves detection of lethal chemical and biological agents and knowledge of how to deal with them, as well as decontamination procedures, medical treatment, and law enforcement.

Progress has been made. For example, Washington, D.C., joined with government units in nearby Virginia and Maryland to establish a "medical strike team" composed of police, fire, and emergency rescue crews who are specially equipped to treat victims of biological or chemical attacks. The team has a decontamination unit that could handle more than 700 people per hour. The team would not be strong enough to cope with a major chemical or biological disaster, however.

U.S. military personnel and civilians who live and work in countries outside the United States could be exposed to attacks with chemical and biological weapons. The government agencies that deal with these dangers have been the subject of criticism in the federal government. In July 1999, the Commission to Assess the Organization of the Federal Government to Combat the Proliferation of Weapons of Mass Destruction issued its report. The commission considered the dangers of WMD overseas and found that these weapons pose "a grave threat to U.S. citizens and military forces" and their allies in many parts of the world. It criticized the overlapping powers of the dozens of agencies that deal with WMD and warned that more effective laws are necessary.

President Bill Clinton agreed that the United States needed to do more to provide protection against chemical and biological weapons. For fiscal year 2000 (October 1, 1999–September 30, 2000), he recommended an expenditure of $1.4 billion for protection against a chemical or biological attack. This amount would double the funds spent for this effort in fiscal year 1999. Plans include strengthening the local response teams who would be the first emergency personnel at the scene of a chemical or biological attack in American cities.

One analyst noted that an effective chemical attack on military personnel and civilians who had taken personal protective measures would require at least 100 to 1,000 times as much chemical agent as an effective chemical attack on a similar group of people who are unprotected. Effective protection measures, then, could reduce the damage of an attack or prevent an individual, group, or nation from undertaking the attack in the first place.

CHAPTER 3

PAST USE OF CHEMICAL AND BIOLOGICAL WEAPONS: THE LEGACY OF NATIONS

Today, the mass killing of human beings by chemical and biological weapons is the subject of many novels, films, and television programs. The use of sarin in the Tokyo subways and the potential danger posed by Iraq's possession of such weapons have drawn public attention to the topic. Fear about the possible use of chemical and biological agents in war is not a recent phenomenon, however.

Early Uses

The use of poisons in warfare has ancient roots. Age-old texts tell of using poisons from plants and animals to make weapons more lethal, and old Indian, Chinese, and European military books mention the use of poisonous smoke based on alkaloids and toxins. In about 2,000 B.C. in ancient India, armies used smoke screens to hide their movements, *incendiary* devices to cause fire, and toxic fumes to cause sleepiness among enemy soldiers. In 600 B.C. in Greece, Athenians won a battle by poisoning the River Pleisthenes, the source of drinking water for the defenders of a beseiged city. According to Thucydides, a Greek historian, the Peloponnesians tried to overcome the town of Plataea with sulfur fumes in the fifth century B.C.

In Asia and Europe, many military forces used corpses of dead animals and humans to poison wells and other sources of drinking water. Another practice involved catapulting the bodies of people and horses who had died from disease into besieged cities, or leaving diseased bodies in areas about to be occupied by the enemy. In 1346, during the siege of the town of Kaffa, a Genoese trading outpost in the Crimea (part of the Ukraine), the Tartar army hurled dead victims of the bubonic plague, which had spread westward from China, into the town by means of trebuchets—medieval devices used for throwing heavy stones. The plague spread throughout the town, and survivors fled by ship to Italy, carrying the plague with them. This incident helped spread the Black Death that killed millions of people in Europe and Asia.

In 1763, British forces in North America may have used a biological weapon against some Native Americans. Sir Jeffrey Amherst, the British commander-in-chief, supposedly suggested that blankets infected with smallpox be distributed to hostile Native American tribes. A few months later, many deaths from smallpox occurred in Indian tribes in the Ohio area. Historians disagree about whether Amherst's plan caused the smallpox epidemic, however.

But chemical and biological weapons had little military significance until the twentieth century. Generally, not enough chemical or biological agents were available to make them a central part of military operations, so they were used in specific situations in a limited way. When advances in technology made it practical to use chemical weapons for military purposes, these agents came into use on a large scale in warfare.

The technology was largely a product of the growth of industrial society. The industrial demands of the nineteenth century led to increased production of chemicals, including chlorine and phosgene. Military officials, political leaders, and others were aware that these chemicals, which were created for industrial purposes, could be used as weapons of war. Fears about the possible destruction associated with chemical weapons led to the Hague conferences of 1899 and 1907 that banned the use of asphyxiating gases in war (see Chapter 6).

World War I

World War I marked the first major use of chemical weapons in wartime. Opposing armies had reached a stalemate—neither side could advance without suffering great losses. So the soldiers dug in and built trenches. Hoping to break this deadlock, Germany launched an attack on April 22, 1915, near Ypres, Belgium, with 150 tons of chlorine gas. The gas was released from cylinders in the form of a cloud along a 3.5-mile (6-kilometer) front. This was the first toxic gas attack in the history of warfare. Germany and France had used gas attacks in World War I before the battle at Ypres, but these attacks had involved harassing, not lethal, agents.

At Ypres, wind carried the gas into the trenches of Allied soldiers, resulting in an estimated 15,000 casualties, with about 5,000 deaths. Allied soldiers panicked and retreated from the area of attack—they were unprepared for this new kind of warfare. The exact number of casualties at Ypres and other areas where gas was used is a matter of dispute, in part because of propaganda—false claims spread by the warring nations.

The attacking Germans suffered casualties too, when pockets of gas hit them when they moved forward or when the wind changed direction. Germany was unable to take advantage of the success it had that day at Ypres because it was unprepared. It lacked the resources to make a breakthrough. Pockets of gas and a Canadian and French counterattack during the night also slowed the German advance. The Allies—Britain, France, and other countries—quickly brought in new soldiers and took steps to protect their troops from gas attack, such as providing them with respirators (gas masks).

In a few months, the Allies had their own supply of gases to use against the enemy. By the end of May 1915, the situation had changed little. Soldiers on both sides used gas masks for

In World War I, a German officer and his men advance through a cloud of phosphene gas that they set off themselves to provide cover as they moved toward British trenches.

protection. Attacks with chlorine, phosgene, and other chemicals became more frequent, and gas warfare spread to other combat areas.

On July 12, 1917, the Germans introduced mustard gas against British forces, again at Ypres. Mustard gas attacks the skin and disables anyone who comes in contact with it (see Chapter 1). In the first three months after mustard gas was

The horses and soldier in this French resupply team in World War I are both wearing gas masks.

introduced, this chemical weapon resulted in more than 14,000 British casualties. Like the 1915 chlorine attack, the mustard attack caused many casualties but did not break the stalemate. Both sides had to develop protective clothing, in addition to gas masks, to provide safety from the mustard gas attacks.

Chemical warfare proved not to be decisive in the outcome of World War I. Sometimes, the side that first used the poison gas was not prepared to use force and take advantage of its initial success. Sometimes, it had no knowledge of the effects of the gas on the opposing soldiers. Each side also feared that the opposing forces would launch a counterattack with gas weapons.

By November 1918, when World War I ended, the warring nations had spent huge amounts of money on chemical weapons research. Gas warfare neither broke the deadlock associated with trench warfare nor won battles, but it had a devastating psychological impact on the soldiers—it wasn't easy to forget the choking and the blisters. Some experts have stated that no reliable data are available to determine the number of casualties. According to one estimate, poison gases accounted for the death of fewer than 1 percent of the men who died in battle during the entire war. But chemical weapons—mainly chlorine, phosgene, and mustard gas—may have taken a million soldiers out of action and killed 100,000 people. Although most of the casualties were military personnel, some were civilians. These weapons forced government officials and others to be concerned about the possibility of the production and use of more deadly chemical weapons.

Biological warfare agents were used only in a limited way in World War I. German saboteurs who carried out destructive actions against enemy forces secretly spread a bacterial disease called glanders to kill enemy horses. These animals were necessary for the movement of supplies and for other transport purposes.

Between World Wars I and II

Once chemical weapons had proved successful in producing casualties, they continued to be used. In 1919, chemical weapons may have been used in a minor way during the Russian Revolution by White Russian forces. They may also have been used in 1925 by the Spanish in Morocco and in the early 1930s by the Chinese.

In 1935–1936, Italy used chemical weapons on a large scale in its invasion of Abyssinia (now Ethiopia). Mustard gas was sprayed from aircraft to produce injuries among soldiers, interfere with military operations, and hurt morale. The chemical attacks caused thousands of casualties. Because Ethiopia did not have chemical weapons, it could not respond in kind. Experts differ regarding the importance of the use of poison gas to the Italian victory in the war.

Experts disagree about whether minor chemical weapons use occurred in Europe in World War II. It is clear that the Allies—Great Britain, France, the United States, and the Soviet Union, among others—and the Axis—Germany, Japan, and Italy—did not use them in Europe, however.

The use of chemical weapons in World War I marked a breakdown in the customary avoidance of poison in war. After that breakdown, the nations worked to establish an international standard. The Geneva Protocol, signed in 1925, forbade "first use" (initial introduction) of chemical weapons (see Chapter 6). In 1939, at the beginning of World War II, Great Britain, France, and Germany agreed to abide by the Geneva Protocol of 1925. In 1943, President Franklin D. Roosevelt pledged that the United States would not initiate the use of chemical weapons in the war.

A number of explanations have been put forward to account for the failure to use chemical weapons in World War II. Great Britain may have had concerns about preserving its empire. Although it took steps to protect people in the British Isles from chemical attack, it feared that if chemical weapons were used, Japan might attack India. At that time, India was a British colony and had little defense against chemical warfare. Great Britain had another reason for not using chemical weapons. It feared that once chemical warfare began, it would have to redirect its limited resources from its other war-related efforts. Many analysts believe that if Germany had been strong enough to invade Great Britain, British Prime Minister Winston Churchill would have used chemical weapons to defend his country and avoid defeat.

Although Germany had vast stores of chemical weapons, it chose not to use them. On June 6, 1944, when Allied forces launched the D-day invasion—a massive attack on German-occupied territory in France—Germany did not use chemical agents. Even when Allied forces fought their way through Germany itself, Hitler did not use chemical weapons.

Some historians believe that German leader Adolf Hitler thought that the Allies had superior airpower that could reach German cities. As the war continued, German airpower declined so that Germany would have been at a disadvantage in a war with chemical weapons. If the Allies had used air raids to attack German cities with chemical weapons, Germany would not have had enough gas masks to supply its entire civilian population.

Possibly, Hitler may have thought that his enemies had chemical weapons that were superior to those of Germany. If Germany started to use its chemical weapons, it would lose out in the long run. Because the United States had failed to *ratify* (approve) the Geneva Protocol of 1925, Hitler may have thought that President Roosevelt was free to use chemical weapons.

Some experts argue that producing and using vast amounts of chemical weapons would have placed a great strain on the German military and the economy. Some historians also mention that Hitler had personal reasons for not using chemical weapons. As a soldier in World War I, he had been temporarily blinded by British mustard gas.

Finally, it is certainly possible that many nations didn't use chemical and biological weapons for legal and moral reasons. Revulsion, or a strong dislike, about the use of poison in war has deep and ancient roots that extended into the twentieth century.

World War II was a truly global conflict. Although Europe avoided chemical warfare, Asia did not. Japan used chemical weapons against China from 1937 to 1945. Japan's use of chemical weapons was tactical and limited. Japan also used biological weapons to attack Chinese troops and civilians. Between 1940 and 1944, Japan attacked at least 11 Chinese cities with biological weapons.

As early as 1930, the Japanese Imperial Army had established Unit 731 for development of biological weapons. Unit 731 used at least 3,000 prisoners of war—Chinese, Mongolians, Soviets, Americans, British, and others—as human guinea pigs to test agents of biological warfare, including anthrax toxin. Estimates of the number of prisoners of war killed in the experiments range from 1,000 to 3,000.

After World War II

Since World War II, some nations have used—or have been accused of using—chemical or biological weapons. The areas of the world in which such charges have been made are Korea, Yemen, Vietnam, Laos, Cambodia, Afghanistan, Iraq, and Iran.

In 1951 and 1952, during the Korean War, the governments of North Korea and the People's Republic of China accused the United States of using biological weapons to spread diseases such as plague, cholera, and typhus among North Korean and Chinese forces. North Korea also charged that U.S. forces had used chemical weapons against North Korean soldiers. The United States denied the charges. A majority of United Nations (UN) members did not support North Korea and China.

In 1963, Egypt intervened in a civil war in Yemen on the side of the Republicans. The opposing Royalists and their supporters charged that Egypt had used chemical weapons. Reporters and other observers found evidence of such use, but Egypt denied the charges.

During the Vietnam War, the United States used irritant agents and *herbicides,* substances that destroy plants. The United States argued that international law permitted such use. The United States also supplied irritant agents to the army of the Republic of Vietnam. The U.S. government contended that such agents were necessary to support military actions. It argued that because these weapons were nonlethal, they were humane.

The U.S. government used tear gas in Vietnam in much the same way as U.S. police do to control riots and maintain

These aerial photographs show the effects of herbicide use on mangrove forests in Vietnam. Herbicides were not sprayed on the forest pictured at the top, but they were used in the forest on the bottom, where they caused extensive damage.

public order. U.S. armed forces used tear gas to clear bunkers and caves of suspected enemy soldiers, attack targets, and engage in operations in areas where the enemy had seized hostages.

During the Vietnam War, the United States admitted that it used herbicides in Vietnam, Laos, and Kampuchea (formerly Cambodia). From 1962 to 1971, U.S. military personnel sprayed 18.85 million gallons (71 million liters) of herbicides over Vietnam. The United States relied on herbicides to destroy vegetation, and as a result, the enemy had fewer places to hide easily to attack American troops. The *defoliants,* which caused the leaves of plants to fall off, were used to protect the boundaries of bases and allow military forces to discover enemy routes and hiding places. The herbicides also destroyed crops and thus deprived the enemy of food. Although herbicides were designed for use against military sites, they damaged the country's farming industry.

One of these herbicides was *Agent Orange.* Many members of the U.S. armed services who were exposed to Agent Orange claimed that it caused medical problems that developed later, such as cancer and birth defects in their children. Although no connection between Agent Orange and these medical problems has been established beyond doubt, the manufacturers of Agent Orange have paid out $180 million to the affected veterans.

The use of chemical agents in the Vietnam War was met with much criticism within the United States as well as in other countries. Some critics charged that these substances were chemical weapons covered by the Geneva Protocol. Others argued that the use of herbicides was militarily ineffective. Scientists concluded that the herbicides had long-term environmental and public health consequences. In 1967, thousands of scientists signed a petition to President Lyndon Johnson calling for an end to the use of antipersonnel and anticrop weapons in Vietnam. Many scientists also criticized any action that contributed to chemical and biological warfare. In 1969, the UN General Assembly adopted a resolution declaring that the Geneva Protocol prohibited the use of any type of chemical or biological weapon. The United States argued that international law does not forbid the use of riot-control agents and herbicides.

In the late 1970s, the use of chemical weapons again became a subject of attention in Southeast Asia. Refugees reported that Vietnam began using chemical weapons in Laos and Kampuchea soon after the Vietnam War ended. Journalists described this substance as *yellow rain* because the refugees said that rockets or sprays created clouds that had a yellow color. In addition, the falling particles sounded like rain.

Chemical weapons were also an issue in Afghanistan, where Soviet military forces fought the mujahideen rebels. Between 1979 and the mid-1980s, Afghan refugees claimed that the Soviets were using biological weapons against the rebels. Journalists made similar reports.

In 1981, the United States charged that the Soviet Union used, or let others use, chemical weapons in Laos (1975–1981), Kampuchea (1979–1981), and Afghanistan (1979–1981). The United States claimed that the chemical agent was yellow rain. A number of scientists and others opposed this charge. Chemist Julian Robinson, sociologist Jeanne Guillemin, and biochemist Matthew Meselson investigated the situation and challenged the U.S. view. They concluded that the yellow rain was not the result of a chemical attack, but rather of natural developments—specifically, bee droppings. The issue is still disputed.

In the 1960s, Iraq began to use chemical weapons in warfare. In 1965, reports of Iraqi use of chemical weapons against Kurdish rebels in Iraq appeared. In the 1980s, Iraq's use of chemical weapons became widely known. Iraq invaded Iran in 1980 and seemed to be winning at first. But Iran went on the offensive, regaining the territory it had lost and even establishing footholds in Iraq. In 1982, Iraq began using chemical

Iraq used nerve gas against the Kurds in northern Iraq in 1988.

weapons to prevent advances by Iran's armed forces and to relieve its desperate military situation.

Iraq's use of chemical weapons continued throughout the war. In 1987 and 1988, Iran began to fight back and seems to have used chemical weapons against Iraq. According to experts, the specific chemical agents used by Iran are unknown, but analysts believed that by 1988, Iran could produce hydrogen cyanide, phosgene gas, or chlorine gas and was attempting to produce nerve gas.

Iran claimed that Iraq's chemical attacks caused 12,600 casualties. According to a 1984 UN inspection team, Iraq used mustard gas and nerve agents. In their book *Gene Wars: Military Control Over the New Genetic Technologies*, authors Charles Piller and Keith Yamamoto note that this is "the only authoritatively verified use of nerve gas in history and the first involving mustard gas since World War II." In one incident in 1988, Iraq used a mixture of mustard gas and nerve gas against the Kurds in the city of Halabja in northern Iraq, reportedly killing 5,000 people and injuring thousands of others.

Tests and Accidents with Chemical and Biological Agents: Too Many Secrets

To have effective chemical or biological warfare agents, governments need to know that the agents will work properly. Testing the weapons supplies this knowledge. The tests may cause unintentional problems because of poor planning or failure to carry out the tests correctly, however. Accidents may occur, with unintended consequences.

In the 1950s and 1960s, the U.S. Army secretly tested biological weapons over American cities and other areas. The experiments were conducted to evaluate how vulnerable the United States was to attack by biological weapons. These tests exposed millions of Americans to biological agents and chemical particles. According to some scientists, the tests may have been harmful, but the army contended that the biological agents were never a danger to people, animals, or plants.

One of the commonly tested substances was the bacterium *Bacillus subtilis*, a biological simulant—an agent that is supposedly an imitation of a lethal biological weapon. Some scientists believe simulants can cause disease, however. The U.S. Army often refers to this bacterium as BG (which stands for *Bacillus globigii,* another name for the bacterium). BG is not known to be a major threat to health, but it can cause infections in people who are weakened by other conditions—immune deficiency conditions such as AIDS, wounds following trauma, and recent surgery, for example. The Army tested BG over cities and other areas. Although it stopped testing bacteria and chemical agents over residential areas in 1969, it continued outdoor spraying with simulants at the Dugway Proving Grounds in Utah.

The U.S. Army also conducted tests of biological weapons over other areas, including San Francisco, Washington, D.C., Key West, and Panama City (Florida), plus parts of Alaska and Hawaii. The experiments included spraying bacteria in the New York City subway system and along the Pennsylvania Turnpike. Between 1949 and 1969, the Army sprayed a total of 239 populated areas in the continental United States with bacteria. These facts were not made known to the public until a committee of the U.S. House of Representatives revealed the information in 1977.

In 1968, 6,000 sheep died in Skull Valley, Utah, which is 60 miles (96 kilometers) from Dugway. The Army has never accepted responsibility for this event. It denied that it used nerve gas, a charge made by some scientists, but, in 1969, it paid $1 million in damages to the owners of the sheep. According to Army records, several ranchers in the area became sick at the time, but the Army concluded that nerve gas did not cause their illnesses.

Strange incidents have occurred in the Soviet Union too. The reported accidental release of anthrax in the city of Sverdlovsk in April 1979 led to debate about the illegal manufacture of biological weapons. The reports came from individuals who had left the country. At that time, anthrax caused at least 66 deaths in the Sverdlovsk area.

Soviet officials said that the anthrax cases resulted from natural causes—the consumption of contaminated meat. The United States pointed to extensive Soviet military involvement in the clean-up operation at the Microbiology and Virology Institute in Sverdlovsk. It charged that the Soviets had violated the 1972 Biological Weapons Convention (BWC), which

In 1968, 6,000 sheep died in Skull Valley, Utah, 60 miles from Dugway Proving Grounds, where tests of biological and chemical agents were conducted. The U.S. Army never accepted responsibility for the deaths of the sheep. However, in 1969, it paid $1 million in damages to the owners of the sheep.

outlaws biological weapons, although the Soviet Union had ratified this agreement (see Chapter 6).

In 1981, the administration of President Ronald Reagan accused the Soviet Union of violating weapons agreements, including the Geneva Protocol and the BWC. Specifically, it claimed that the Soviets or their allies used yellow rain–type toxins in Southeast Asia and Afghanistan, that the outbreak of anthrax in Sverdlovsk occurred at an illegal biological weapons facility, and that the Soviets were developing new biological weapons based on recombinant DNA techniques.

Dr. Ken Alibek (formerly Kanatjan Alibekov) defected to the United States from the former Soviet Union in 1992. He held a high position in a Soviet civilian weapons program. He reports that Russia continues to conduct research on the development of new biological agents.

In 1992, a year after the Soviet Union broke up into fifteen independent countries, Russian President Boris Yeltsin confirmed that the incident at Sverdlovsk resulted from an accidental release of anthrax bacteria from a military research facility. He admitted that the Soviet Union had violated the BWC and issued a decree banning the continuation of the biological weapons program.

In 1998, Dr. Kanatjan Alibekov (now known as Ken Alibek), who was second-in-command of a branch of the civilian biological weapons program in the Soviet Union until his defection to the United States in 1992, reported that the Russians still carry out research on the development of new biological agents. Some U.S. intelligence analysts believe that elements of the old Soviet biological program continue, but experts are far from certain that these include the development of offensive weapons. Russian officials deny that Russia is continuing the program.

Recent Developments

In recent years, the threat of chemical and biological warfare has come from the poorer, developing nations of the *Third World,* not the major powers, such as the United States and Russia. In the 1960s, only five countries were believed to have chemical weapons. Today, there may be more than 20, which is about three times the number of nations that have nuclear weapons. Most of the increase had occurred in the Middle East and East Asia. According to U.S. intelligence estimates, about 17 countries now have biological weapons, including China, Egypt, Israel, Iran, Iraq, Libya, North Korea, Russia, Syria, and Taiwan.

Most of the countries that are developing chemical and biological weapons are located in politically unstable areas of the world. In these regions, conflicts with other nations have led to war in the past and could easily lead to war in the future. The United States views some of these countries, such as Iran and Iraq, as international outlaws.

CHAPTER 4

PROLIFERATION: WHY DO NATIONS OBTAIN CHEMICAL AND BIOLOGICAL WEAPONS?

The *proliferation,* or rapid increase, of chemical and biological weapons was a feature of the twentieth century. When Germany began using chemical weapons in World War I, other countries responded in kind. After the war ended, other countries acquired chemical weapons. According to British intelligence sources, 13 nations had offensive chemical weapons by 1938.

For the most part, chemical and biological weapons were not used in World War II, although the major countries that were involved in the war possessed these weapons (see Chapter 3). After the war, there was no race to develop such weapons. In 1980, about 12 countries were known to have or suspected of having chemical weapons. Today, the number may be more than 20. The number of countries known or suspected of possessing biological weapons grew from one—the Soviet Union—in 1980, to about 17 by 1999. The fear is that more nations will want to acquire chemical and biological weapons.

A nation that wants chemical and biological weapons can easily get them. For example, in the 1970s, Iraqi leaders decided to develop an arsenal of chemical and biological weapons. The country built plants to produce chemical weapons, relying on imported technology and materials from Western countries.

Saddam Hussein, the Iraqi president, has stated that he would use chemical and biological weapons in response to a nuclear attack.

On April 2, 1990, Iraqi President Saddam Hussein said, "We do not need an atomic bomb. We have the 'dual chemical.'" It was not clear whether his reference to the "dual chemical" applied to mustard gas and nerve agents or to binary weapons. But he definitely viewed chemical agents as weapons that could be used to kill people.

Reasons for the Proliferation of Chemical and Biological Weapons

Many factors contribute to the proliferation of chemical and biological weapons. The most important factors are cost, military advantage, security and deterrence, political advantage, bureaucracy, and the weakening of norms. Often, combinations of two or more of these factors may result in proliferation.

Cost

Compared to nuclear weapons—and even conventional weapons—chemical weapons are inexpensive to produce. And biological weapons cost even less than chemical weapons. A nation without great economic and technical resources could easily produce chemical and biological weapons.

As mentioned in Chapter 1, many of the needed chemicals are used in industry and are therefore readily available at relatively low cost, either from foreign countries or from domestic sources. As Third World countries modernize, they often develop industries that make dual-use products. They can then use the same materials for both military and commercial purposes. Even medical laboratories and hospitals may serve as sources of supplies for the manufacture of biological weapons.

Scientists, physicians, and engineers from developing countries often gain research experience in more technologically sophisticated countries. The growing number of trained technicians makes it easier for smaller countries to develop biological agents.

Military Advantage

Under certain conditions, having chemical and biological weapons gives a country a military advantage. When Germany launched a surprise gas attack at Ypres in 1915, it created panic among enemy forces (see Chapter 3). Germany was not able to take advantage of this form of warfare because it was unprepared, but several military benefits are usually associated with the possession of chemical and biological weapons.

A government that possesses chemical and biological weapons has a powerful tool to use against rebel forces that challenge its authority within its own country. If the rebel forces are concentrated in a particular region, they make an easy target. And if they belong to a particular ethnic group with strong antigovernment feelings, moreover, the government may have few constraints about using the weapons against civilians—other than harsh criticism by other countries.

Opposing military forces must devote time and energy to protecting themselves with gas masks, specially treated clothing, extra medical personnel, and emergency equipment. Soldiers in advancing armies must wear protective gear, so they move slowly and cannot operate at peak efficiency. When the soldiers are not wearing gas masks and other protective gear, they are exposed to chemical and biological weapons.

Another military advantage for a country involves the kinds of weapons that are used. A country with chemical and biological weapons may deliberately use those weapons that

In hot climates, soldiers may be able to wear masks and special clothing for only short periods of time.

are likely to produce injuries that require medical treatment but do not cause death. It may do so because medical treatment requires substantial use of money, personnel, and supplies.

The use of chemical weapons has a devastating effect on the morale of soldiers under attack and also produces panic among those forces. In addition, chemical and biological weapons may affect personnel at supply depots, airfields, and command and control posts, thus complicating the enemy's movements and effectiveness.

Unlike conventional weapons, moreover, most chemical and biological weapons do not cause physical damage. Once the fighting is over, the country that uses chemical and biological weapons does not need to devote tremendous resources to rebuilding. In many cases, it must decontaminate areas, but the costs of decontamination are not likely to be as high as the costs of reconstruction.

During the Iran-Iraq War, Iraq used chemical weapons to its military advantage. Iran was not immediately able to retaliate in kind, largely because Iranian forces had no protective equipment and did not possess these kinds of weapons. Iraq's successful use of chemical weapons in that war sparked a build-up of chemical and biological weapons by other nations.

Security and Deterrence

Nations desire military power for many reasons. Some leaders hope to use it to conquer other countries and get more land. Many leaders want military forces to be strong enough to defend their country if another country attacks it. Some countries adopt a policy in which their armed power is so strong that their enemies refrain from attacking them for fear of devastating consequences. This is what *deterrence* means.

A classic example of deterrence is the nuclear arms race between the former Soviet Union and the United States during the Cold War. The Cold War was a period of intense distrust and suspicion that lasted from the end of World War II in 1945 until the breakup of the Soviet Union in 1991. Both nations built huge nuclear arsenals that could easily be launched. To deliver these nuclear weapons to their targets, they constructed bombers, intercontinental missiles, and nuclear-powered submarines. Each country understood that even if it was essentially destroyed by a sneak attack from the opposing side, it would still have enough nuclear weapons to wipe out its enemy. This knowledge prevented either side from engaging in nuclear war.

Some countries manufacture chemical and biological weapons so that fear of retaliation will prevent an enemy country from using such weapons against them. Germany did not use chemical weapons during World War II, although it had them. It feared that the Allies would use them more effectively if Germany used them first.

Deterrence may have prevented Iraq from using chemical and biological weapons, but no one can be sure. In August 1990, Iraq invaded Kuwait, a neighboring country. That same month, President George Bush, who opposed the Iraqi intervention, declared that "the use of chemical weapons [in the Persian Gulf area] . . . would be intolerable and would be dealt with very, very seriously." The United States and its allies then began a military buildup in the Persian Gulf area.

In December 1990, U.S. Secretary of Defense Richard Cheney said that if Iraqi President Hussein were foolish enough to use WMD, the U.S. response would be overwhelming and tremendously destructive. Some experts interpreted these comments to mean that the United States would use nuclear weapons if Iraq used chemical weapons against soldiers of the United States and its allies.

Under UN guidance, U.S. and allied forces bombed military installations in Iraq and won a decisive military victory. But Iraq did not use its chemical weapons. Iraq had Scud missiles, long-range missiles that could hit allied forces in neighboring countries. These missiles were capable of carrying chemical and biological warheads, but the missiles Iraq launched against Israel contained conventional explosives rather than chemical and biological weapons.

Political Advantage

During the Cold War, both superpowers—the United States and the Soviet Union—sought allies throughout the world. The superpowers could provide security guarantees as well as economic and military assistance. After the end of the Cold War, the situation changed. Countries that were formerly dependent on the superpowers felt free to act independently of the major powers. Some countries chose WMD as a policy option, in part to replace security guarantees withdrawn by the superpowers.

Bureaucracy

Once a government bureaucracy—a unit of government that performs a specific task—is formed, there is often a tendency for it to continue even when the reasons for its formation no longer exist. The government agency has particular views and interests that are often difficult to control.

After World War I, for example, the Chemical Warfare Service of the U.S. Army wanted to maintain chemical weapons. It did not support U.S. ratification of the Geneva Protocol of 1925, an international agreement that attempted to control chemical weapons. The chemical industry also objected to the Protocol, which might have weakened support for maintaining a supply of chemical weapons. In countries that have recently begun to develop chemical weapons, similar government agencies may also be exerting their influence in programs that favor chemical and biological weapons.

Weakening of Norms

Many countries, including the United States, did not act when Iraq used chemical weapons against Iran. The conflict seemed to affect views of governments about chemical weapons in a major way. Governments became favorably disposed to having their own chemical weapons.

For its part, the United States was more concerned about the revolutionary government of Iran and the spread of

Islamic fundamentalism—a belief in strict adherence to a set of principles—than it was about Iraq. Iran was hostile to the United States. In 1984, the United States renewed diplomatic relations with Iraq that had been broken off. Taking the view that "my enemy's enemy is my friend," it downplayed the Iraqi use of chemical weapons.

Iraq, the Persian Gulf War, and Chemical and Biological Weapons

In response to the Iraqi invasion of Kuwait in August 1990, nations opposed to the invasion began a military buildup. In 1991, a group of countries, led by the United States, decided to use military force to restore Kuwait's independence. This conflict became known as the Persian Gulf War. The United States committed nearly 700,000 troops, with other countries contributing 200,000 troops.

U.S. soldiers in Saudi Arabia conduct a chemical decontamination exercise in November 1990.

The United States and its allies knew that Iraq had chemical and biological weapons, and soldiers of U.S. and British forces in the Persian Gulf area were immunized against anthrax. Intelligence agencies underestimated Iraq's ability to deliver biological and chemical weapons—a fact that became known when inspectors from the United Nations Special Commission (UNSCOM) investigated Iraq's chemical and biological weapons programs after the war ended. As a result of the defection of two high-ranking Iraqi officials in 1995, Iraq admitted that it had produced the biological agents anthrax, botulinum toxin, and aflatoxin (a fungal poison).

Before the Persian Gulf War, U.S., British, and Israeli intelligence agencies failed to recognize that Iraq was able to produce the rockets, bombs, and warheads capable of carrying biological and chemical agents. Also, the United States may have underestimated the amount of botulinum toxin that Iraq had by a factor of at least a thousand and the amount of anthrax by at least a factor of eight. According to statements made by Iraqi officials, Iraq made enough botulinum toxin from 1989 to 1991 to wipe out the Earth's population several times over. Iraqi officials also admitted making enough anthrax and *Clostridium perfringens* (a biological agent that causes gangrene and, in aerosol form, can cause severe gastric effects) to kill or maim billions of people.

Nearly 80,000 of the 697,000 Americans who served in the Persian Gulf during Operation Desert Shield and Operation Desert Storm, the allied military effort in the Persian Gulf War, suffered from illnesses, including memory loss, headaches, fatigue, and joint pain after the war. The condition came to be known as *Gulf War syndrome*. Claims were made that the illnesses resulted from exposure to chemicals in the war, but the cause is as yet unknown.

Iraq possessed large quantities of chemical and biological weapons, but it did not use them. It is not known for certain why Iraq accepted defeat rather than use these weapons, but experts have offered a number of possible explanations. First,

Iraq may have feared that the United States would respond with nuclear weapons. Second, Iraq's major means of delivering the chemical weapons had been eliminated with the destruction of its airpower and artillery. Third, President Hussein may have believed that the measures taken by allied forces to protect themselves against chemical or biological attack were effective. And fourth, Iraq experienced a collapse of its command and control system.

Although Iraq did not use chemical or biological weapons in the Persian Gulf War, many nations feared that it would use them in the future. Under terms that ended the Persian Gulf War in 1991, the UN Security Council created UNSCOM in an effort to make Iraq give up its WMD. UNSCOM inspectors examined documents, conducted on-site inspections of illegal weapons sites, and succeeded in destroying forbidden weapons.

The Iraqi government tried to hide evidence of chemical and biological weapons from the inspectors. On August 3, 1998, Iraq announced the end of its cooperation with the inspectors. In December 1998, the United States and Great Britain launched a four-day air attack against Iraq after President Hussein prevented UNSCOM from proceeding with its efforts to deprive Iraq of its WMD. In 1999, the future of inspections was tied up with negotiations over ending UN economic *sanctions* against Iraq. (Sanctions are penalties for violating an agreement.) The resolution of the problem of Iraq's WMD seemed uncertain.

CHAPTER 5

TERRORISM: HOW MUCH OF A PROBLEM IS IT?

In an age in which individuals and groups can obtain or manufacture chemical and biological agents relatively easily and cheaply, *terrorism* is already a reality. Aum Shinrikyo carried out a terrorist attack with sarin in the Tokyo subways. Terrorism is difficult to define in a way that is acceptable to everyone. According to the U.S. State Department, terrorism is "premeditated, politically motivated violence perpetrated against a noncombatant [a person who does not engage in fighting] target by subnational [belonging to a smaller group rather than a whole nation] or clandestine [secret] state agents, usually intended to influence an audience."

No matter how terrorism is defined, the political aspect is a key difference between terrorism and other criminal activities. Terrorists claim that they commit violent acts for what they see as a noble political cause, such as forming an independent state from the part of a country where an ethnic group currently lives, ending racism, supporting freedom and religious causes, aiding oppressed people, or fighting a corrupt government. The following section presents some specific examples of terrorism involving chemical and biological weapons that occurred in the last part of the twentieth century.

Terrorist Acts

In recent decades, terrorists have resorted to such acts as hijacking airplanes, bombing places where innocent civilians live or work, kidnapping civilians or public officials, committing murder, and robbing banks. Individuals and groups have also engaged in, threatened, or planned acts of terrorism involving chemical and biological agents. These incidents include the following events:

- In 1972, law-enforcement officials seized 80 pounds (36 kilograms) of typhoid bacteria cultures from an American fascist (far right) organization called the Order of the Rising Sun. The group planned to contaminate the water supplies of Midwestern cities with these bacteria.

- In 1978, a Bulgarian intelligence agent in London used an umbrella to fire microscopic pellets containing ricin into the body of Georgi Markov, a Bulgarian defector. Markov died from the poison.

- In 1978, Europeans in at least three countries became sick after eating citrus products, such as oranges, that had been imported from Israel. The products were contaminated with mercury. A group that called itself the Arab Revolutionary Army Palestine Command claimed responsibility for the act, saying that it wanted to damage the Israeli economy.

- In 1980, police in Paris raided the apartment of the Red Army Faction, a terrorist group. They discovered a small laboratory that contained a culture of the bacterium *Clostridium botulinum.*

- In 1984, two members of a cult led by Bhagwan Shree Rajneesh put salmonella bacteria in salad bars in the town of The Dalles, Oregon, near where the cult was located. After eating food from the salad bars, 751 people became ill. The cult members wanted to prevent citizens from voting on whether to force the cult to leave the area.

- In 1988, tiny traces of cyanide were found in two Chilean grapes. In response to this discovery, the United States recalled all Chilean fruit in the United States—U.S. officials took it off the market for several weeks. The incident severely damaged the Chilean economy.
- In May 1994, the judge in the case involving the 1993 bombing of the World Trade Center said that the defendants might have placed sodium cyanide in the explosives on purpose. When the bombs exploded, the cyanide gas would have killed hundreds—perhaps thousands—of people. But instead of vaporizing, the chemical burned, so it did not have the intended effect.
- In 1995, Larry Wayne Harris, a former member of a white supremacist group, ordered three vials of freeze-dried bubonic plague bacteria through the mail from the American Type Culture Collection, the largest distributor of microorganisms in the world. The company notified the Federal Bureau of Investigation (FBI) because it became suspicious of the number of phone calls Harris had made asking about the shipment. He served only a short sentence for mail fraud because he had sent false information through the mail. At the time, there was no law against the purchase of the bacteria.
- In 1995, Thomas Lewis Lavy was charged with attempting to smuggle 130 grams (4.6 ounces) of ricin from Alaska into Canada with intent to use the toxin as a weapon. He told police that he was planning to use the ricin to poison coyotes on his Arkansas farm. U.S. and Canadian law-enforcement officials believed that Lavy had no reason to have ricin unless he planned to use it for criminal purposes.
- In March 1995, two members of the Minnesota Patriots Council, a right-wing militia, were convicted for planning to use ricin to kill federal tax officials.
- In March 1995, Aum Shinrikyo, a Japanese cult, released sarin gas in the Tokyo subway system, killing 12 and injuring more than 5,000 people (see Introduction).

- On April 24, 1997, a package containing a petri dish holding a red substance labeled "Anthrax" arrived in the mail at the Washington, D.C., headquarters of B'nai Brith, a national Jewish organization. Police closed off a city block and quarantined workers to prevent the spread of disease. Officials later determined that the package did not contain anthrax. The incident was a cruel prank.

The damage in terms of injuries and deaths resulting from a major terrorist chemical or biological attack could be greater than the number of casualties produced by these incidents. To get an idea of the level of casualties that can result from such a catastrophic incident, we can examine an event that involved chemicals but was not a terrorist act—namely, a disaster that occurred in Bhopal in Central India in 1984. After toxic gas leaked from a Union Carbide plant that manufactured insecticides, a cloud formed over the city. Because there was no wind, the cloud did not break up and remained at ground level. The incident resulted in at least 2,500 deaths and approximately 125,000 injuries. Some of the injured people will require medical treatment for the rest of their lives. The disaster in Bhopal was the worst industrial accident in history.

Imagine some hypothetical terrorist cases involving chemical and biological agents that could easily lead to catastrophic results. Terrorists could place poisonous chemicals in the water supply of a city, drop anthrax spores in a city's subway system with the intention of spreading the anthrax throughout the system, or place sarin near the airshaft of a big office building. Terrorists could make a new disease using genetic engineering, so that vaccines and antidotes would not exist.

Are terrorists likely to commit a major chemical or biological attack that kills hundreds, thousands, or even millions of people? The experts differ in their answers and offer the following arguments.

In February 1999, authorities evacuated a three-block area in midtown Atlanta after receiving a report that a package containing anthrax had been delivered to the offices of NBC News.

Yes, Terrorists Will Use Chemical or Biological Weapons to Commit Mass Murder

Terrorists have already used chemical and biological weapons. People who are faithful to a cause that they believe to be more important than their own lives would not hesitate to use such weapons to produce catastrophic results. Consider these three reasons.

1. *Many terrorists want to kill large numbers of people.* Although the number of terrorist incidents has declined in recent years, the incidents have become more deadly. Recent terrorist incidents are designed to cause as many civilian casualties as possible in order to make a political point. For example, a few particularly gruesome incidents

that produced high numbers of casualties include the following:

- 1988 explosion of the Pan Am jetliner over Lockerbie, Scotland
- 1993 bombing of the World Trade Center in New York City
- 1995 bombing of the Federal Building in Oklahoma City
- 1995 sarin attack in Tokyo
- 1997 suicide bombing in Israel

The explosion of the Pan Am jetliner killed 270 people—259 passengers plus 11 people on the ground. The bombing of the World Trade Center, which left a crater 200

An injured victim of the World Trade Center bombing in February 1993 receives emergency assistance.

by 100 feet (60 by 30 meters) wide and five stories deep, killed 6 people and wounded 1,000 others. Authorities estimated the damage at nearly $1 billion. Ramzi Yousef, the leader of the group convicted of the bombing, hoped to topple one of the buildings, which might have killed up to 250,000 people—about the same number who live in Louisville, Kentucky. The 1995 bombing of the Federal Building in Oklahoma City left 168 people dead and 500 wounded. The 1995 sarin attack in Tokyo killed 12 people and injured more than 5,000 others (see Introduction). The 1997 suicide bombing on a busy shopping street in Jerusalem took the lives of 7 people (including the 3 Palestinians who set off the explosives) and wounded about 170 others.

Some individuals believe that terrorists wish to avoid a large number of casualties because they want to influence public opinion. They do not want to alienate people whose political support they think they ultimately need. According to this viewpoint, terrorists commit violent acts so that people will pay attention to their political goals. Killing innocent civilians does nothing to win the minds and hearts of people. But recent acts of terrorism show that this assessment may be wrong. "Instead of wanting to get a lot of people to watch, there are those who now want a lot of people dead," says one expert on terrorism.

A close look at recent acts of terrorism reveals individuals and groups who are so enthusiastic and committed to a cause that they are willing to commit acts that are often viewed as irrational. Aum Shinrikyo was a religious cult with a weird notion about the need to promote death in order to bring about Armageddon. Yousef, who hated the United States, planned to destroy dozens of jumbo jets over the Pacific. Fanatics, or extremists, who are committed to a cause, whether it is political or religious, often have feelings of self-righteousness—they think they are better than other people. The emotions of terrorists sometimes allow them to feel virtuous rather than guilty when they cause what they see as a grand event, such as the murder of large numbers of innocent people.

True, it would be difficult for terrorists acting on their own to commit a catastrophic terrorist act that claims the lives of thousands. But the case of Aum Shinrikyo shows that relatively small groups without state sponsorship could produce catastrophic results. With the support of a government, the terrorists would have the necessary financial backing and perhaps the technical expertise. Nations have been willing to engage in terrorist acts in the past. North Korea tried to assassinate the entire cabinet of South Korea in 1983, and Libya was behind the blowing up of a U.S. plane in 1988. So some countries will use chemical and biological weapons if they think they can get away with it.

The new terrorists are prompted by religious fundamentalism or by ethnic or group hatred. Some religious fundamentalists are convinced that their violent acts are justified by God. In 1995, a Jewish fundamentalist murdered Israeli Prime Minister Yitzhak Rabin. The killing, torture, and other atrocities committed in ethnic or group conflicts, such as those that occurred in the 1990s between the Serbs and the Kosovars in Yugoslavia, and the Hutus and Tutsis in Rwanda, demonstrate that people of one group sometimes have such contempt for people of a different group that they see those people as less than human. That was the view of Nazis in their dealings with Jews, and the slaughter of other groups goes on, sometimes because of events that occurred centuries ago.

2. *Terrorists can manage to obtain and use chemical and biological weapons successfully.*
   It is true that many terrorist groups don't have the support of a country and don't have enough money to buy powerful weapons. They may steal the weapons or commit robbery to get money. But chemical and, especially, biological

weapons are relatively inexpensive. A 1969 report by a UN panel compared the cost of attacks with different kinds of weapons. According to the report, "in a large-scale operation against a civilian population, casualties might "cost" about $2,000 per square kilometer (about 0.4 square miles) with conventional weapons, $800 with nuclear weapons, $600 with nerve gas weapons, and $1 with biological weapons." Although the actual cost may change over the years, the ratio will remain about the same.

Today, it is relatively easy to learn about chemical and biological weapons. Much of the information is publicly available, and some of it, including formulas for nerve gas, mustard gas, and herbicides, has been published in scientific journals. The U.S. Defense Department has declassified the formula for VX, the powerful nerve agent, and a foreign military institute has published a book that provides a detailed description of how to launch a gas attack.

The web sites on the Internet are even more accessible. Several books available on the Internet, including *The Anarchist's Cookbook* and *The Terrorist Handbook*, provide detailed information about deadly weapons. Few people are needed to produce these weapons, and many weapons can be manufactured in a small space.

If the terrorists had scientific skills, they might be able to develop weapons themselves. By taking vaccinations or antidotes, they could avoid being injured or killed by the agents they were setting loose. If they lacked the technical expertise to develop some of these weapons, they could hire scientists to do it for them. Some countries, such as Iran, have hired scientists from the former Soviet Union to help with their chemical and biological weapons programs.

Thanks to developments in science and industry worldwide, terrorists have many materials from which to choose. Advanced industrial societies have the latest chemical and biological products. Since the end of World War II, moreover, developing countries have built factories to make these materials.

Some harmful agents are dangerous to manufacture, but others are not. Terrorists could purchase a chemical such as phosgene from a chemical or agricultural supply company and avoid the problem of manufacturing the necessary chemicals. Delivery of these weapons does not require the long-range bombers, ballistic missiles, and submarines needed to carry nuclear weapons. A truck, car, or helicopter would do the job, or possibly, as in the case of the Aum Shinrikyo attack in Tokyo, the terrorists could simply carry plastic bags of the poisonous agent.

Governments in industrial societies have eagerly increased trade with developing nations and supported the modernization of traditional societies. Developing nations now have universities, scientific institutes, and chemical plants that allow them to improve their economies. With so much economic strength, technical talent, and knowledge, terrorists now have worldwide access to the materials that produce chemical and biological weapons.

Although some nations have established export controls on chemical and biological agents and equipment that can be used in the manufacture of WMD, these controls are difficult to administer, partly because these materials are used for commercial, as well as military, purposes. Hundreds of biological culture collections in the world are available in nations with no export controls. And, of course, illegal dealers can supply these biological agents for a price.

In addition, the revolution in genetic engineering has given terrorists access to new pathogens for which there is no known antidote. These disease-causing organisms could produce a major epidemic that would take the lives of millions of people.

Large quantities are not necessary. A speck of VX that would fit on the head of a pin is enough to kill a human being. Four tons of VX released in aerosol form in a crowded city could kill several hundred thousand people. Only about 100 pounds (48 kilograms) of anthrax spores in aerosol form could cause the same number of casualties.

3. *Terrorists who use chemical and biological weapons can escape detection by law-enforcement officials more easily than terrorists who use conventional weapons.*

In recent years, terrorists have committed a number of violent acts for which no individual or group has taken responsibility. Such incidents include the downing of the Pan Am jetliner over Scotland in 1988, the Oklahoma City bombing in 1995, and the bombing at the 1996 Summer Olympics in Atlanta. Unlike terrorists who engage in violent activity because they want to make a political statement, the criminals involved in these incidents were "silent terrorists." They wanted to create fear—to make people feel that they are never really safe.

True, some of these terrorists were captured. Not all of these criminals are caught, however, and some commit many terrorist acts before they are arrested. Some members of Aum Shinrikyo engaged in many terrorist acts, including murder and the release of biological agents, but many of its members avoided detection for years.

Terrorists may discover that chemical and biological weapons offer useful ways to avoid detection. They could inject viruses causing diseases into pharmaceutical products and nobody might ever know who did it. Or they could release anthrax on a plane and be nowhere near the aircraft when the passengers begin to feel ill.

*   *   *

The advances in science and the changes in the economy in recent decades that make it possible for terrorists to use chemical and biological weapons should not be ignored. Today, terrorists have a sense of self-righteousness about the catastrophic acts they commit.

No, Terrorists Will Not Use Chemical or Biological Weapons to Commit Mass Murder

Although chemical and biological weapons give terrorists the chance to cause massive casualties, it is unlikely that they will want to do this—or succeed if they try to do it. Since nuclear weapons were first used in 1945, experts warned that terrorists could—and would—obtain and use these weapons. But that disaster has never occurred.

The suggestions that millions of deaths will occur as a result of terrorist chemical and biological attacks are far-fetched. This is not to say, however, that terrorists will avoid using chemical and biological agents. They have already used them, and they will probably continue to do so. But they will not cause the kinds of catastrophes that some analysts predict for three major reasons.

1. *Many terrorists do not want to kill large numbers of people.* Any act involving mass destruction would hurt innocent civilians and decrease popular support of the terrorist cause. The harm to civilians may be in the form of death or injury or the contamination of areas for long periods of time. Terrorists are interested in gaining popular support, and being branded as mass murderers is not going to win friends and influence people. Mass destruction would also lead to a law-enforcement crackdown. And the toxic substances they use may unintentionally kill the terrorists themselves.

   Most acts of terrorism are symbolic—they are likely to generate publicity but not to cause death. Only about 20 percent of terrorist incidents involve fatalities. Although terrorists could use explosives to kill large numbers of people, such acts are rare. One analyst studied more than

10,000 incidents committed by international terrorists between 1968 and 1998 and reported that fewer than a dozen involved more than 100 deaths.

2. *It's not easy to commit mass murder with chemical and biological agents.*
Large amounts of chemical weapons are needed to kill many people. The larger the quantities terrorists need, the greater the chance that they will be discovered before they have carried out their attack. Also, the chemical or biological agents may not work as planned. The effective dispersal of chemical and biological agents depends on factors such as temperature and other weather conditions. Terrorists have to work in secret, and they do not have precise information about weather patterns. They also lack the manufacturing and storage facilities available to governments and legitimate businesses. As a result, they are likely to find that their chemical and biological agents are degraded, even if they are dispersed.

In particular, terrorists would find biological weapons difficult to control. Dr. Philip Brachman, who worked on the original anthrax vaccine research in the 1950s, said that it's very difficult to put *Bacillus anthracis* into the form of a cloud. As he pointed out, it needs to be in tiny droplets and the wind currents must be exactly right to get it to "float for miles."

Even with conventional explosives, terrorists have been known to blow themselves up accidentally as they manufacture the explosives. Consider the technical problems that Aum Shinrikyo faced. The plant that produced the sarin never operated properly, and the nerve agent that the group used was impure. Instead of dispersing sarin with sprayers, the terrorists relied on a relatively ineffective method—puncturing plastic bags that contained the liquid. The agent evaporated too slowly to cause a large number of deaths. And in another incident, Aum was reported to have released anthrax bacteria on two occasions without harming anyone.

Contaminating water supplies can be difficult too. Most water-treatment systems use filtration and chlorination to kill disease-carrying microorganisms. The treatment systems would probably destroy the biological weapons agents. Because the quantity of water in most water-supply systems is so great, terrorists would need large quantities of the biological agent to prevent or minimize the effects of its being less concentrated. It would be impractical for terrorists to use large quantities of a biological agent to avoid this problem, or they might be noticed by outsiders.

In addition, terrorists may not be able to get reliable information necessary to produce chemical and biological agents. Although it may be easy to get information about chemical and biological agents or weapons on the Internet, the terrorist cannot be certain of the accuracy of the information—particularly when it comes from questionable sources. One expert noted that *The Anarchist's Cookbook* contains numerous factual errors, including the wrong chemical formula for alcohol.

The building of chemical and biological plants would be too expensive for terrorist groups. So, too, would the acquisition and storing of the materials. In considering their methods, terrorists might decide that conventional weapons would achieve their objectives more effectively. And explosives make a "bang" that attracts attention. Explosives kill and injure people just as cruelly as chemical and biological weapons do, and sometimes they are even more inhumane. It is true, however, that chemical and biological weapons would probably cause more fear and panic than explosives.

3. *Terrorists who use chemical or biological agents have a high risk of being caught and punished.*

Terrorists are often under police surveillance as a result of past errors or informants. They depend on a small number of trusted associates. In producing chemical and biological weapons, they do not have the "quality control" that a commercial manufacturer has. They cannot be certain about the technical ability of their members. It is also difficult to actually commit an attack with biological weapons before law-enforcement agencies find out about plans to make such an attack and take action to prevent it.

Anyone involved in carrying out a chemical and biological attack faces severe penalties. If a country sponsored the terrorism, other nations would probably respond with strong military action. It would be dangerous for a government to undertake such a risky project, because if law-enforcement authorities from the country that had been attacked identified the offending nation, it would risk the possibility of revenge by the victims.

Any group responsible for supplying the equipment or precursor chemicals to terrorists would be subject to prosecution or punishment too. In 1996, Congress passed the Antiterrorism and Effective Death Penalty Act, which limits the availability of many pathogens that could be made into offensive weapons. The U.S. Department of Health and Human Services issued rules that went into effect on April 15, 1997, regulating the transfer of 36 lethal viruses, toxins, and other biological agents by mail. Governments are devoting huge resources to programs that prevent terrorist acts and bring the people who engage in such acts to justice.

*   *   *

Terrorist acts will no doubt occur and will claim lives. At times, terrorists will be ingenious in the kinds of acts they commit. But it is unlikely that they will have the knowledge, skill, or even desire to commit an atrocity of catastrophic proportion through the use of chemical or biological weapons.

CHAPTER 6

ATTEMPTS AT CONTROL: PRACTICAL SOLUTIONS?

Although countries go to war for many reasons, including security, economic gain, prestige, and ideology (a body of ideas), they have sought to limit the devastation produced once military conflict occurs. They have done this by establishing rules, either by custom or *conventions* (formal agreements). Both custom and conventions are based on international law.

International Law: How It Works

International law is the body of rules that are legally binding on nations. It is based on custom, formal agreements, general principles of law recognized by civilized nations, court decisions, and the writings of legal scholars. International law differs from domestic law, which governs a country. In domestic law, law-enforcement officials have the authority and the power to make sure that members of a community abide by the law. International law depends on the willingness of nations to accept its rules. Because it has no power to enforce its rules, some people say that international law has no true legal status. How can we have laws, they ask, if the laws depend on voluntary acceptance rather than on enforcement?

In fact, many nations abide by international law because they believe they will benefit from its rules. For example, nations have sought to minimize the destructiveness of war through international law. They have adopted rules that ban the use of certain kinds of weapons, rules that guarantee fair treatment for prisoners of war and noncombatants, and rules that establish conditions for peace talks.

Although nations have used poisonous weapons in war, as Chapter 3 shows, they sometimes refrained from using them even when they had them. The custom of condemning the use of poison or poisoned weapons in war or inflicting unnecessary suffering has roots based on the practices of different civilizations. In ancient times, Greeks and Romans deplored the use of poisoned weapons as a violation of the law of nations.

In the Middle Ages, Christian thinkers proposed the "just war" theory to evaluate the legitimacy of war. Part of that theory asserts that the conduct of war should be based on the principle of proportionality, in which certain practices and weapons that caused "unnecessary suffering" were condemned. The use of poison was one of the condemned practices. In the sixteenth and early seventeenth centuries, Europeans fought religious wars that took a heavy toll in human life, but they did not engage in widespread use of poisoned weapons because this was believed to produce unnecessary suffering.

In 1625, the Dutch jurist (legal scholar) Hugo Grotius wrote *De Jure Belli ac Pacis* (*The Law of War and Peace*), the first definitive text in international law. The book describes the customary practices of nations and condemns the use of poisons in war as a violation of the law of nations.

As weapons of war became increasingly destructive due to advances in science and technology, nations have resorted to agreements and other measures since the late nineteenth century to limit the devastation that wars can produce. This effort is known as *arms control*. Nations have not sought what pacifists (people who believe that all conflicts should be settled

In 1625, Hugo Grotius, a Dutch jurist, wrote the first book on international law.

peacefully) call for, however. Pacifists seek *disarmament*—the abolition of military forces and weapons.

People who support arms control assume that nations can and will go to war. They believe that nations should be militarily strong enough to defend their territory, foreign policy, and way of life. They feel, however, that arms control reduces the risk of war by easing tensions among rival nations, avoiding arms races, obtaining political or military advantages, reducing damage caused if war occurs, and saving money.

Problems in Arms Control

Development of an effective arms control agreement requires finding solutions to five problems: (1) verification, (2) universality, (3) the wording and clarity of the convention itself, (4) the political will among the parties to enforce the treaty, and (5) sanctions. First, *verification* is the certainty that each party to an agreement complies with the terms of the agreement. To reach that degree of certainty, each party must be able to check that no party to the agreement is secretly violating the agreement. A country that is not following the rules may have an unfair advantage—with possible fatal consequences.

Two nations that suspect each other are somewhat like two people who do not trust each other but agree to meet and not carry guns. If one person secretly has a gun and the other does not, the one without the gun may be killed by the other. In this example, the risk is high for one person. But with chemical and biological weapons, thousands, possibly millions, of people's lives are at stake. If country A gets rid of its chemical and biological weapons to comply with an arms control agreement, but country B secretly stockpiles these weapons, then the security of country A is in jeopardy. If country A has other powerful weapons that could greatly damage country B, the effects might not be so disastrous. Still, country A might be at a disadvantage with respect to country B.

To ensure verification, nations that suspect illegal actions involving the manufacture or acquisition of chemical and biological weapons might conduct a *national technical means of inspection*. This process, which may include several kinds of monitoring procedures, does not require on-site inspection. Various methods include reconnaissance satellites, photography and electronic surveillance, human intelligence (such as spying), and environmental sampling—the testing of air or water near a suspected production facility. National technical means of inspection, however, can provide only limited information about possible storage sites or manufacturing plants.

Countries that wish to undermine the value of national technical means of inspection for chemical and biological weapons could do so with careful planning. It would not be too difficult to build a manufacturing facility that could be undetected. A chemical plant that could produce 100 tons of a classical agent such as phosgene or chlorine would require a space that could be as small as 40 by 40 feet (12 by 12 meters) in size. A bigger facility—one that could manufacture larger amounts of standard chemical weapons—could be built into a mountainside or hidden among buildings used to produce industrial chemicals. Iraq had chemical weapons production and storage sites that U.S. intelligence did not know about until after the United States and its allies defeated Iraq in the Persian Gulf War in 1991.

The production of biological weapons is even easier to hide than the production of chemical weapons. Biological agents require a much smaller and cheaper industrial *infrastructure*. (An infrastructure consists of the basic facilities, equipment, and installations necessary for the operation of a system.) It is not always easy to determine whether a certain biological agent is responsible for an outbreak of disease. For example, a new and deadly strain of "flu" may come from natural sources.

Because some biological agents are quite powerful, a country that wishes to use them in an attack might find that only a few pounds would be needed to cause many deaths. As discussed earlier, it doesn't take many bacteria to kill people. With anthrax, just a few thousand bacteria are enough. Because only days or weeks would be needed to increase the quantity of a biological agent, it would not be necessary to store a large supply of these agents.

On-site inspection is so important because of the nature of the production and storage of chemical and biological agents and weapons. International inspection may not be the perfect way to determine the existence of chemical and biological agents, but it does provide some information. Without going inside, experts may not be able to distinguish between a manufacturing facility that produces vaccines for peaceful purposes and a plant that produces biological agents and toxins for war. It is difficult to hide production of some chemical weapons, such as mustard gas, from equipment designed to detect the gas. Other evidence may also be apparent, such as traces of chemical warfare agents, which may remain even after attempts are made to clean up spills. Inspectors can examine water and soil samples, and the information can be revealing. The area outside suspect buildings may also contain detectable substances, moreover.

It is important, too, for inspectors to evaluate whether chemical or biological weapons are being used in military operations. This is not difficult to determine. The use of these weapons in war leaves many telltale signs, such as corpses with no wounds and soldiers who lose skin when no fire or explosion occurs. Concentrations of chemical residues may be high for days.

Supporters of arms control agreements recognize the difficulty of having agreements that require absolute verification. They argue that verification of chemical and biological weapons can never be perfect, but they contend that the process does not have to be perfect to be successful. It must be good enough to discover any cheating that is significant from a military point of view, and it must prevent any country from thinking it can make chemical and biological weapons without detection.

A second problem concerning the development of an effective arms control agreement relates to *universality*—the application of rules to all countries rather than just a few or even most. Even if the nations that approve an arms control pact are confident that they will all abide by the agreement, they are concerned about countries that do not approve the agreement but may threaten their security. These countries may be just as dangerous as countries that do approve it.

A third problem associated with the formation of an effective arms control agreement involves the wording and the clarity of the convention itself. To finalize an international agreement, diplomats must resolve the conflicts among national and group interests. Diplomats may delete or weaken phrases and provisions in the draft document that are likely to be unacceptable to powerful parties—governments or influential groups with an interest in the agreement.

An agreement may contain wording that protects commercial interests at the expense of strict standards that would strengthen it. Sometimes, the wording is deliberately ambiguous to make the agreement acceptable to countries that might not otherwise support it. Future technological developments may also make the language outdated.

A fourth problem with the development of an effective arms control agreement involves determining whether the parties to a convention have the political will to enforce it. Often, it is difficult to create a sense of unity among countries and convince them to take strong measures against an offending nation. Great economic, cultural, political, and military differences exist among countries. In 1997 and 1998, for example, the United States faced this problem. It requested support from friendly nations for possible military measures against Iraq when that country violated its agreements to allow UN inspection of suspected WMD production or storage sites. Few countries supported the U.S. position.

A fifth problem with the formation of an effective arms control agreement involves imposing effective sanctions. The sanctions must be strong enough to produce compliance with the agreements. Military action is one type of sanction. Economic sanctions such as embargoes (prohibitions on trade) may also be effective.

International Conventions on Chemical and Biological Weapons: What Have They Accomplished?

Countries have conflicting views about the meaning of international agreements on chemical and biological weapons, and supporters of these agreements have had difficulty making them effective. This fact is as true of the Hague Conferences of

1899 and 1907 as it is of the most recent agreement, the 1997 Chemical Weapons Convention (CWC).

Hague Conferences of 1899 and 1907: Pledging Not to Use Poisonous Weapons

The International Peace Conference held in 1899 at The Hague in Holland (the Netherlands) included a declaration entitled "Laws and Customs of War on Land." This agreement affirmed the prohibition against "the use of poison or poisoned arms," which had been viewed as customary international law for many centuries. Twenty-four nations pledged to "abstain from the use of projectiles the sole object of which is the diffusion [spreading] of asphyxiating or deleterious [harmful] gases." A second Hague Conference in 1907 upheld that pledge and added, "It is especially forbidden to employ poison or poisoned weapons."

But the agreements reached at the Hague conferences did not prevent nations from using gas in World War I. Germany, for example, was a party to the convention. Yet it used chemical weapons, as did other nations who took part in the conferences. Germany denied that it violated the Hague conventions, pleading that its first attacks relied on cylinders rather than projectiles. It also asserted that France used chemical weapons first—a charge denied by the Allies. In 1919, the Treaty of Versailles, the peace treaty that marked the end of World War I, included a provision that forbade the use, manufacture, and importation of poisonous gases in Germany. This provision, however, did not prevent Germany from violating the agreement.

Geneva Protocol: Outlawing Chemical and Bacteriological Weapons in War

The great loss of lives and resources in World War I led to a popular movement to reduce the horrors of war. The movement sought to control weapons of war that violated the customs and laws of war. Many people feared that even more horrible weapons could be produced. With the development of aircraft that could fly increasingly long distances, it was clear that chemical weapons could be targeted at civilians in cities as well as troops on battlefields.

In response to the fears about chemical warfare, the United States, the United Kingdom, France, Italy, and Japan pledged in 1922 that they were opposed to the use of chemical weapons in warfare. They called on other countries to support this view. Wording to this effect was included in the Five-Power Naval Limitation Treaty, which was signed at the Washington Conference in 1922. But the treaty never went into effect, because France objected to a provision that dealt with submarines.

The Geneva Conference for the Supervision of the International Traffic in Arms of 1925 was the first major international agreement involving chemical and even biological weapons. The conference was not convened for the purpose of limiting or eliminating the international traffic in arms, however. The conference produced the Protocol for the Prohibition of the Use in War of Asphyxiating, Poisonous, or Other Gases, and of Bacteriological Methods of Warfare, which banned the use of chemical and bacteriological weapons in war. (The term "bacteriological" was used at the time to refer to what is now described as "biological.") Although bacteriological weapons were mentioned in the Protocol, chemical weapons were the concern of the times. Biological weapons were only beginning to be considered as an instrument of modern war.

Nearly one-fourth of the countries that ratified or acceded to the Protocol had two reservations. First, the Protocol would bind them only in dealing with countries that were also parties to the convention. Second, if a country attacked them with chemical or bacteriological weapons, they would be free to respond in kind. For many nations, then, the Geneva Protocol became a no–first-use treaty that legally allowed them to respond to a chemical or bacteriological attack with a weapon used in the attack but not to initiate its use.

Supporters of the Protocol do not claim that it solved all problems related to the use of poisonous weapons in war. But they believe that the Protocol had a positive effect in dealing with the use of chemical warfare agents. First, they say that the Geneva Protocol provided political barriers against the use of chemical weapons in war. An offending nation would have reason to believe that other countries might impose sanctions, such as trade barriers, against it. Countries that were horrified by the use of such weapons might form an alliance against the offending country. Countries that did not ratify the Protocol could face a loss of international prestige.

Second, supporters say that the Geneva Protocol made a powerful moral statement. That is, the use of chemical and bacteriological weapons is so objectionable that any nation using these agents would be viewed as a moral outcast. To the extent that national leaders feel compelled to respect moral concerns, they would be reluctant to disregard these feelings.

Third, the Protocol broadened the meaning of "chemical weapons" by including all chemical weapons, not just projectiles. The Hague Declaration of 1899 had prohibited the use of "projectiles" that contained chemical weapons. As indicated above, Germany argued that it had used cylinders, not projectiles, in World War I, and so claimed it did not violate the declaration.

Fourth, the Geneva Protocol was the first treaty to deal with biological weapons. It set an important precedent—the Biological Weapons Convention (BWC) was not open for signature (ready to be ratified) until nearly half a century later.

Critics of the Geneva Protocol contend that it was a failure. First, the Protocol established no system of verification to make sure that the parties were complying with its provisions. Without the consent of the suspected violator, no inspection team— whether from an international organization or another party to the agreement—could investigate on-site whether a country had violated the Protocol. It was assumed that the first use of chemical or bacteriological weapons would be obvious.

Second, the countries agreed to no–first-use of chemical and bacteriological weapons, but they could legally respond to an attack with chemical weapons. Because nations at war often make charges that cannot easily be verified, one country could falsely claim that it used chemical weapons in response to the acts of another country that had violated the Protocol.

Third, the Protocol dealt with the use of chemical weapons but not with their manufacture and possession. Countries might comply with the terms of the Protocol and still manufacture and store vast supplies of chemical and bacteriological weapons. The manufacture of such weapons by one nation would be bound to lead to production of similar weapons by rival nations. Such was the case in World War II.

Fourth, because the Protocol applied only to those countries that ratified it, universality was a problem. The United States, for example, was not legally bound by the terms of the Protocol for many decades because it did not ratify the Protocol until 1975—50 years after the convention was open for ratification.

Fifth, no provisions explained what the response to violations would be. It was not known whether the parties to the agreement would take military action against offending parties, impose economic sanctions, or simply issue statements of disapproval.

Sixth, there was a lack of clarity about what the Protocol actually covered. Did the agreement limit use of chemical and biological weapons only against humans? Or did it include agents that act against plants and animals? It was not clear what kinds of chemical agents the Protocol prohibited.

During the Vietnam War, the United States claimed that the use of lachrymatory agents and herbicides was legal according to the Geneva Protocol. For the United States, this view was not new. As early as 1930, the country defended the use of tear gas in war by contending that it served a humane purpose. Tear gas was used in peacetime to control civil disturbances, and outlawing its use in war would be wrong.

If the use of chemical and biological agents in warfare is a criterion for judging the effectiveness of the Geneva Protocol, then the Protocol may be said to have been quite successful. True, Italy used chemical weapons in its war against Ethiopia (see Chapter 3). Italy, which had ratified the Geneva Protocol, violated it by using chemical weapons in this case. Italy, however, defended its legal position by asserting that the Geneva Protocol did not prohibit the use of chemical weapons in reprisal against other illegal acts of war. According to Italy, Ethiopia had engaged in such atrocious acts as the torture and killing of military prisoners and noncombatants as well as the use of dum-dum bullets. These bullets expand on contact, producing a deep and wide-open wound. Japan, which had supported The Hague Declaration of 1899 but had not ratified the Geneva Protocol, used both chemical and biological weapons against China beginning in the late 1930s.

Most countries did not use chemical and biological warfare agents, however. Except for Japan's war with China, World War II was fought without the use of chemical and biological weapons.

Biological Weapons Convention:
Banning Possession and Use of Biological Weapons

During the Vietnam War, the United States took steps to outlaw biological weapons. In November 1969, President Richard Nixon declared that the United States renounced biological weapons and that it would destroy all its existing stocks of these weapons. The United States made this move as a matter of its own policy. It was not complying with an international agreement. The Nixon announcement also recommitted the United States to a no–first-use policy for lethal chemical agents and declared that the United States would extend this commitment to incapacitating chemicals. In 1970, the United States included toxins as part of the new policy.

President Nixon may have taken these steps for several reasons. First, he may have been influenced by popular and international criticism of U.S. policy on chemical and biological weapons during the Vietnam War. This statement was a way to express U.S. concern about such weapons. Second, his administration may have believed that biological weapons were of minimal benefit in warfare. Third, he may have thought that advances in biological weapons would not aid more powerful nations that already had superior nuclear and conventional weapons. Instead, they would help smaller powers develop a WMD capability.

In 1972, the BWC (known formally as The Convention on the Prohibition of the Development, Production and Stockpiling of Bacteriological [Biological] and Toxin Weapons and on Their Destruction) was opened for signature. Article I requires the parties "never in any circumstances to develop, produce, stockpile, or otherwise acquire or retain" biological agents or toxins "of types and in quantities that have no justification for prophylactic [preventive], protective, or other peaceful purposes." Unlike the Geneva Protocol, which deals with "first use," the BWC obligates parties to destroy all biological weapons "in any circumstances." Article II obligates parties to destroy all biological weapons they may possess within nine months. Article III prohibits transfer to "any recipient whatsoever" and prohibits assistance to other states or international organizations regarding the manufacture or acquisition of agents, toxins, or means of delivery.

But Article XIII of the convention allows a party the right to withdraw from the convention "if it decides that extraordinary events, related to the subject matter of this Convention, have jeopardized the supreme interests of the country." Article XIII repeats standard language in all post–World War II arms control agreements and demonstrates a common practice of nations.

On March 26, 1975, the BWC went into effect. Within five years, more than 100 nations had ratified it, including the United States. As of October 1999, 144 countries had ratified it.

Although the BWC contains no provisions for verification, it does consider the problem of nations that do not comply with the terms of the agreement. In cases of noncompliance, the parties who believe the rules have been broken may consult with each other. They may also use the procedures found in the

UN Charter relating to countries that violate their obligations. The UN Security Council would then conduct an investigation in which the parties were legally bound to cooperate.

Supporters of the BWC have hailed its strengths. First, the BWC is the first treaty in modern times to prohibit the possession as well as the use of biological weapons. It bans biological weapons of any kind, including weapons developed by genetic engineering. As such, it is a landmark disarmament agreement. Second, it expresses the opinion of many nations that biological and toxic weapons should not be used in war.

Critics point to a number of weaknesses of the BWC. First, like the Geneva Protocol, the BWC contains no provisions for verification of any violations of the agreement. The people who drafted the convention may have felt at the time that there was no way to perform effective verification. Possibly, this absence of verification provisions allowed some nations to ratify the treaty and then violate it without fear of being caught. When the BWC was drafted, technical experts may have believed that verification of biological weapons had too many technical problems to be possible.

Second, the BWC does not ban the possession of biological agents that can be used for peaceful or defensive purposes. Arguably, military forces could develop genetically engineered agents and claim they were doing so as a defensive measure in compliance with the agreement. Because biological agents can reproduce quickly, they are an offensive threat to other nations. The BWC, moreover, does not place specific limits on the biological agents and toxins that may be developed for defensive purposes. Very small quantities of these agents can cause tremendous harm.

The only way to determine whether the purpose of producing biological agents is defensive or offensive is to know the intentions of the country that produces them. It is virtually impossible, however, to find broad agreement about evaluating a nation's intentions. One country's statement of its noble intentions may be viewed by another country as a lie. To a great extent, the BWC depends on the goodwill and self-interest of the parties to abide by its provisions.

Third, the BWC does not limit research on biological weapons, the manufacture of necessary production equipment, or the training of armed forces to deal with biological weapons. The agreement, moreover, does not include *confidence-building measures*—procedures such as information exchange and routine inspections that nations could take to reduce the fears of their possible adversaries.

Advances in biotechnology, such as genetic engineering, have complicated the BWC. These advances have increased the number of biological agents that can be used as weapons. In the 1960s and early 1970s, military and scientific authorities believed that it would be difficult to use biological agents on the battlefield because of problems of production, storage, and transfer. This type of problem is not new. Even before the 1970s, advances in science affected international agreements. The Geneva Protocol prohibited bacteriological weapons. But in 1925, microorganisms such as viruses and the rickettsia bacteria were unknown, so the Protocol could not ban them.

The BWC calls for review conferences every five years. Since 1986, the parties at review conferences have agreed to two sets of confidence-building measures. These measures are intended to make a country's activities relating to biological weapons, including defense efforts, more apparent to everyone. The parties to the BWC are not simply recommending inspections. They are negotiating a legally binding protocol to the BWC that will create a regulated system for improving confidence-building. The negotiations involve declarations of activity as well as a detailed program of on-site activities, including visits, investigations, and challenge inspections.

In recent years, the potential use of smallpox as a biological weapon has become a subject of speculation in high levels of government. According to a report in the *New York Times* in June 1999, a secret U.S. government investigation completed in 1998 concluded that Iraq, North Korea, and Russia are probably concealing the deadly smallpox virus. Smallpox, which killed an estimated 500 million people in the twentieth century, has been eradicated worldwide. In 1996, the World Health Organization (WHO), the UN agency responsible for maintaining health standards, recommended that all nations destroy their stocks of the smallpox virus by June 1999—a position supported by the United States.

On April 22, 1996, however, President Clinton reversed this policy and agreed to delay destruction of the virus. Two factors influenced his decision—fear of the potential use of the virus by other countries and a report from the National Academy of Sciences indicating that the virus would speed up the development of new medical treatments. On May 24, 1999, WHO voted to hold on to existing stocks until as late as 2002 because it wanted to permit research on new treatments and develop a better vaccine against smallpox.

Chemical Weapons Convention: Formalizing Inspection

As with biological weapons, some countries voluntarily decided to give up chemical weapons without being required to do so by international agreement. Great Britain decided to destroy its chemical weapons in 1956. The United States stopped production of chemical weapons in 1969. It resumed production of binary weapons in 1987, but it ended the program in 1990.

Negotiations on a major chemical weapons agreement began in 1968 at a meeting of the UN Eighteen-Nation Committee on Disarmament. In the following years, many countries submitted working documents and draft conventions. The use of chemical weapons in the Iran-Iraq War of the 1980s gave the talks a sense of urgency. In 1992, negotiators reached a final agreement.

The Chemical Weapons Convention (CWC) creates a taboo about chemical weapons in the manner that the BWC does about biological weapons. Under the CWC, each party to the agreement undertakes never to develop, produce, otherwise acquire, stockpile, or retain chemical weapons, or transfer (directly or indirectly) chemical weapons to anyone; use chemical weapons; engage in any military preparation to use chemical weapons; and assist, encourage, or induce, in any way, anyone to engage in any activity prohibited to a country that is a party to the convention. In addition, each party agrees to destroy the chemical weapons it owns or possesses or that are located in any place under its jurisdiction or control; destroy all chemical weapons it abandoned on the territory of another country that is a party to the convention; and destroy any chemical weapons production facilities it owns or possesses or that are located in any place under its jurisdiction or control.

The CWC seeks to abolish offensive chemical weapons capabilities for all countries that accept the convention. The treaty establishes inspection procedures and sets up the Organization for the Prohibition of Chemical Weapons (OPCW). The treaty allows countries to conduct research to develop, test, and maintain essential items, such as gas masks and antidotes. It gives countries ten years to destroy their chemical weapons and provides that international inspectors monitor the destruction process.

The CWC is the first arms control treaty that widely affects the private sector. The inspection provisions were written with the input of the chemical industry. In this way, inspection of chemical plant facilities would be permitted but confidential commercial information would be kept out of the hands of inspectors to ensure that it would not fall into the hands of competitors. Inspectors want to make certain that the facilities are being used only for civilian applications. The inspectors examine specific chemicals that have military use. Chemicals that have dual use are also monitored. Companies that produce, process, consume, import, or export these chemicals in quantity must make annual declarations about these activities.

Countries that are not parties to the CWC are not permitted to obtain some of the controlled chemicals. Finally, countries are obligated to enact domestic legislation that makes the acquisition of chemical weapons a crime. The treaty was signed

PROPERTY OF
ROLF IOWA SCHOOLS

by 130 countries in Paris on January 12, 1993 and entered into force on April 29, 1997. As of July 1999, 126 countries had ratified the CWC. The United States ratified it on April 25, 1997.

Supporters of the CWC make several arguments. First, the CWC strengthens norms against the use of chemical weapons in war. Norms do play a role in foreign policy to limit the horrors of war. Since the end of World War II, for example, the norm against the use of nuclear weapons has worked effectively to prevent those weapons from being used in war. To say that norms are important does not mean that they are not violated, but they do play a role that should not be ignored.

Second, the CWC is sufficiently verifiable to discover violations. No arms control agreement is perfectly verifiable, but the CWC provides enough safeguards to prevent cheating. For example, it allows short-notice challenge inspections that make violations likely to be discovered.

A treaty member may request inspection of a country that it suspects is violating the CWC. Inspectors must be permitted to reach any inspections site within 12 hours. The country must permit inspectors to enter the facility within 4 ½ days of their arrival and must give them 84 hours to investigate the charge. Inspectors may perform aerial observation of the site; take soil, air, and other samples around the site perimeter; and take samples within the site.

Third, the CWC is an effective international agreement because it establishes a new international body (the OPCW) to address any concerns about compliance, imposes costs on countries that do not join the CWC by subjecting them to trade restrictions, and requires countries to destroy their vast chemical stockpiles. These features show much improvement over the Geneva Protocol.

Fourth, the CWC will strengthen U.S. national security by reducing the likelihood that chemical weapons will be used in war. Moreover, even if a country does maintain some chemical weapons, the United States will have sufficient conventional weapons to counter any threat that nations make against it. In addition, the United States has nuclear weapons as a safeguard defensive measure.

Fifth, the CWC will strengthen the security of small powers that are particularly vulnerable to attacks from neighboring countries of similar strength. In case of an attack with chemical weapons, they can call on other countries that are part of CWC to assist them.

Critics of the CWC make several points. First, verification is not possible. Because many components of chemical weapons have dual uses, it is not possible to have an effective inspection system that can provide assurances that these

In 1996, a worker under the supervision of United Nations inspectors takes apart a fermentation vat in Iraq that can be used to make biological weapons.

In 1996, a United Nations worker in Iraq destroys growth media that could be used to produce biological weapons.

components will not be diverted for purposes of building chemical weapons. Countries, consequently, could easily cheat. In this regard, the experience of UNSCOM inspections is illustrative of the problem. Since the aftermath of the Persian Gulf War, UNSCOM has had thousands of inspectors searching for illegal biological and chemical weapons. Iraq was still able to hide limited quantities of such weapons from inspections that are far more intrusive than anything permitted under the CWC (see Chapter 4).

Second, countries most at risk are small powers that live up to CWC provisions. It would not take a vast supply of chemical or biological weapons to cause immense damage. Rogue nations that do not comply with international agreements, such as Iraq, North Korea, Iran, and Libya, pose a great danger to their neighbors and would not live up to the CWC.

Third, Iraq's use of chemical weapons against Iran in the 1980s was a violation of the Geneva Protocol, to which Iraq was a party. UN inspectors verified that chemical weapons had been used. Yet other countries did not come to the assistance of Iran. If nations will not come to the assistance of a country attacked with chemical weapons, then how would they ever expect countries to come to their assistance when their neighbors merely produce those weapons?

Fourth, the treaty would be costly. It would establish an unnecessary international bureaucracy that would be expensive. It would, moreover, require costs imposed on the chemical industry that would be burdensome.

Fifth, countries that do not ratify the treaty will find ways to get around the trade restrictions that are formally applied to them. They could purchase chemicals from other nonsignatory nations, develop their own industries to produce these items, or obtain them on the black market.

Other Means of Control

If nations are not successful in getting rules adopted or in having countries abide by the rules that they have created, they may act on their own. Diplomacy, export controls, security assurances, sanctions, and even military intervention may not effectively eliminate chemical and biological weapons. But individual nations are not helpless when it comes to the control of these agents. Using national technical means of inspection, they can monitor the production of chemical and biological weapons without on-site inspection. Intelligence agencies can engage in a variety of activities, including investigations of trade with other countries, monitoring published information, questioning defectors, and spying.

Some countries have implemented export controls on chemical and biological agents. Since 1984, the Australia Group, an informal suppliers' organization that was formed as a result of the use of chemical weapons in the Iran-Iraq War, has had as its goal the coordination of national export controls relating to chemical and biological weapons. This group has sought to prevent the spread of chemical and biological components that can be used to make weapons, including chemical precursors, dual-use equipment, and microorganisms and toxins that could be used for weapons production.

The United States has enacted legislation and adopted regulations to limit the ability of governments, groups, and individuals to produce chemical and biological weapons. The Export Control Act of 1979 and Executive Order 12735 (November 16, 1990) on Chemical and Biological Weapons Proliferation require companies to obtain export licenses on controlled commodities, including chemical or biological weapons–related items. The Chemical and Biological Weapons Control and Warfare Elimination Act of 1991 requires the Secretary of Commerce to establish and maintain "a list of goods and technology that would directly and substantially assist a foreign government or group in acquiring the capability to develop, produce, stockpile, or deliver chemical or biological weapons." Exporters must obtain export licenses when sending such items to specified countries. As indicated in Chapter 5, however, export controls are difficult to administer because the agents and equipment may be used for both commercial and military purposes.

The United States no longer manufactures chemical or biological weapons, so the export of these materials from the United States is not a concern. But stopping the export of products that could be used to make those warfare agents *is* a problem, because many of those materials have applications in commercial enterprises.

Nevertheless, countries determined to get the necessary components to produce chemical and biological weapons have been able to do so by relying on their own internal resources. After the Australia Group barred the export of precursor chemicals to Iraq, that country produced them domestically, relying on technology it had secured from many sources. One analyst observed that nonproliferation efforts actually accelerated Iraq's construction of a local base for the production of chemical weapons!

Before trade regulations such as export controls were strictly enforced, a country seeking to acquire chemical and biological weapons could easily obtain them. Iraq had a biological weapons program by 1974 and probably earlier—certainly before 1979, when Saddam Hussein came to power. Iraq once purchased strains of anthrax and botulinum toxin from a biological supply firm in Maryland, and obtained equipment for processing chemical and biological agents from Italy, Switzerland, and Germany. Before the Persian Gulf War, 50 companies in 5 Western countries and India allegedly sold precursor chemicals and technology to Iraq for use in its chemical weapons program. At the time, all these countries, including the United States, had export-control laws that were all bypassed to some extent.

Other countries in addition to the United States have enacted legislation to tighten up access to dangerous biological agents. In the United Kingdom, for example, the Biological Weapons Act of 1974 makes it a criminal offense to develop, produce, stockpile, acquire, or retain any biological agent or toxin or means of delivery. A person who violates the law is subject to a penalty of life imprisonment.

The United States enacted important laws designed to prevent the acquisition and use of chemical or biological warfare agents by states, groups, or individuals. The Biological Weapons Act of 1989 makes it a federal crime to knowingly develop, manufacture, transfer, or possess any biological agent, toxin, or delivery system for use as a weapon. The Antiterrorism and Effective Death Penalty Act of 1996 strengthens the Chemical and Biological Weapons Control and Warfare Elimination Act of 1991 to cover individuals or groups who attempt or even threaten to develop or use a biological weapon. The law gives the Centers for Disease Control and Prevention (CDC), an agency of the Department of Health and Human Services, the responsibility to create and maintain a list of biological agents that potentially pose a severe threat to public health and safety. The law also gives the CDC authority to institute a procedure that controls the transfer and use of such agents.

The Defense Against Weapons of Mass Destruction Act of 1996 requires that the Secretary of Defense take immediate action to respond to terrorist incidents and to assist emergency-response agencies on the state and local level. An amendment to the Defense Authorization Act for fiscal year 1997 provides $100 million for strengthening these emergency-response agencies. Since then, Congress has provided additional funds for these agencies.

In addition to congressional action, the U.S. president has issued directives relating to chemical and biological weapons. In June 1995, President Clinton issued Presidential Decision Directive (PDD) 39 (*United States Policy on Counterterrorism*), which specifies the responsibilities of federal agencies in the management of crises. In May 1998, he issued PDD 62 (*Combating Terrorism*) and PDD 63 (*Critical Infrastructure Protection*). PDD 62 established a National Coordinator for Security, Infrastructure Protection, and Counterterrorism. PDD 63 authorized the FBI to set up a National Infrastructure Protection Center that would provide warnings to public and private operators of essential government and economic elements.

*   *   *

The control of the use of chemical and biological weapons creates problems that are more complex than those created in the control of nuclear weapons. But nations increasingly recognize the dangers of chemical and biological weapons proliferation and provide evidence that they are working to strengthen both international conventions and their own technical means to minimize the associated dangers.

CHAPTER 7

THE FUTURE: HOPE OR DESPAIR?

The development and use of chemical and biological weapons in the twentieth century provides enough evidence to be pessimistic about the future. Scientists have invented chemicals that can be converted from peaceful and commercial uses into deadly weapons of war. Medical researchers and an astonishly innovative bioengineering industry have fashioned vaccines and antidotes that have given life and hope to people who in earlier centuries would have died from particular ailments. But the new products create extraordinary possibilities of catastrophic loss of life through deliberately planned and human-controlled diseases that take the lives of millions of people.

One could be pessimistic that the forces of modernity in science and technology will lead to doom and despair. A pessimistic view of the future could also focus on the use of chemical and biological weapons in war. World War I saw the beginning of chemical weapons in modern war. After the war, Italy used mustard gas against Ethiopia, and Japan attacked China with both chemical and biological weapons. The Iran-Iraq War of the 1980s may have marked a renewal in the use of chemical weapons for warfare. As a result of this war, nations of the world have begun to view the use of chemical weapons as a possibility. About 20 countries feel so strongly about the possibility that they will be the targets of chemical weapons that they have begun to acquire chemical weapons of their own, and perhaps 17 nations are now working on or acquiring biological weapons. Proliferation continues, particularly in parts of the world that are politically unstable. And the danger that these weapons will fall into the hands of terrorists is always present.

It is not only the technology that poses dangers—it is the purposes to which technology can be used for war that is cause for alarm. Wars are horrible social practices and take many lives. But what is rather new in modern times is that war is becoming more barbaric in the sense that civilians, rather than armed forces, are becoming targets of warfare. In World War I, the ratio of military to civilian casualties was about 90 to 10. Today, that figure has been reversed: for every 10 military casualties, there are on average 90 civilian deaths. The goal in many modern wars, such as in Bosnia, Rwanda, and Kosovo, is the killing of civilians. Chemical and biological weapons, which are indiscriminate in their targets, serve the cause of the new barbarism.

But optimists have reasons for hope too. Sometimes, nations do not use WMD even when they have some reason to do so. In 1945, the United States used atomic bombs twice to end the war in Japan. From 1945 to 1949 it had a monopoly of nuclear weapons, but it did not use them. Nor in later years did any of the nuclear powers, including the Soviet Union and China. The United States did not use nuclear weapons when masses of Chinese troops entered the Korean War, and the Soviet Union did not use nuclear weapons when it suffered setbacks in the war in Afghanistan. Indeed, the striking fact about the historical record is the nonuse of such weapons.

Similarly, with a few minor exceptions, chemical and biological weapons were not used in World War II. They were not used in the Persian Gulf War, either. And enemies of the United States, such as Libya and Iraq, did not employ them against

American targets in the United States. To be sure, enemies of the United States engaged in other violent practices, such as Libya's involvement in the downing of a Pan Am airliner.

The Cold War was fought without chemical and biological weapons too, although debate continues about the use of herbicides and riot-control weapons by the United States and possible use of yellow rain by the Soviet Union in Afghanistan and Southeast Asia. The United States and the Soviet Union built up huge arsenals of biological and chemical weapons, but neither side used them against the other. And both have destroyed or are committed to destroying their stockpiles of these weapons. There are lingering suspicions about the extent of the destruction and even about the integrity of the commitment, however.

Nations have taken practical steps to deal with chemical and biological weapons. They have increased defensive measures to protect against chemical and biological attack. They have improved procedures to deal with emergencies in case of an attack by these weapons either by a country or by terrorists. And they have enacted laws that provide tough penalties against individuals involved in producing or otherwise acquiring the components to make these weapons.

Perhaps most significantly, they have begun to reestablish norms against these weapons by strengthening international conventions. The BWC and the CWC are two cases in point. Few people would believe that the mere signing of a convention is sufficient to end the threat of biological and chemical weapons. But there is hope that nations will be willing to provide effective inspection procedures and take some risks for strengthening international safeguards in these matters. One could, moreover, be reasonably optimistic that the BWC will be strengthened in the coming years.

So there is reason for pessimism and optimism. Is the glass half full or half empty? The answer will be found in the decisions and practices of political leaders and citizens in many nations.

GLOSSARY

aerosol—a suspension of small, fine particles, in a liquid, solid, or gas

Agent Orange—an herbicide used by the United States during the Vietnam War

anthrax—an infectious disease of animals that can be transmitted to human beings

antidote—a remedy that counteracts the effects of a poison

arms control—agreements and other measures that nations adopt to limit the devastation that wars can produce

asphyxiation—suffocation

bacteria (singular, *bacterium*)—single-cell organisms that carry out a wide range of biochemical processes and may be useful or harmful to humans

binary weapon—a chemical weapon composed of separate containers to isolate two substances that are dangerous when combined

biological warfare—the intentional use of microorganisms or toxins to produce death or disease in humans, animals, or plants

blistering agent—a toxic substance that causes wounds to the skin and mucous membranes. This substance is also known as a vesicant.

blood agent—a chemical substance absorbed into the body through inhalation that interferes with the transport of oxygen around the body and damages body tissues

botulinum toxin—a poison produced by the bacterium *Clostridium botulinum*, which is one of the world's most toxic substances

botulism—a disease caused by food that contains botulinum toxin

chemical warfare—the intentional use of toxic substances resulting in death or injury

chlorine—a choking agent that can lead to death

choking agent—a chemical substance that acts by inflaming the lung tissue so that increasing quantities of fluid enter the lungs from the bloodstream and choke the victim

collective protection—the establishment of areas that are free from harmful chemical or biological weapons

confidence-building measure—a procedure such as information exchange or routine inspection that nations can take to reduce the fears of their possible adversaries

convention—a formal agreement

conventional weapons—weapons other than chemical, biological, and nuclear weapons, such as guns and tanks

corrode—wear away gradually

cruise missile—a vehicle carrying a warhead that is guided automatically or by distant human control

culture—a population of microorganisms prepared in a nutrient medium

defoliant—an herbicide that causes leaves of plants to fall off

deterrence—a policy in which the armed power of a country is so strong that its enemies will refrain from attacking it for fear of the consequences

disarmament—the abolition of military forces and armaments

disperse—to spread widely or scatter. (The act of spreading a material is known as dispersal.)

dual-purpose chemical—a chemical agent that has both commercial and weapons-related uses

epidemic—an outbreak of a contagious disease

fermentation—a process by which a chemical reaction splits complex organic compounds into relatively simple substances

fungi (singular, *fungus*)—organisms that are responsible for the decay and decomposition of organic matter

genetic engineering—the process of manipulating the genetic material (DNA) of cells

Gulf War syndrome—illnesses, including memory loss, headaches, fatigue, and joint pain, that some military personnel claimed resulted from exposure to chemicals in the Persian Gulf War

harassing agent—see irritant agent

herbicide—a substance used to destroy plants

incendiary—capable of causing fire

infrastructure—the basic facilities, equipment, and installations necessary for the operation of a system

international law—the body of rules that are legally binding on nations

irritant agent—a chemical substance that affects the senses. It is also known as a harassing agent.

lachrymator—a chemical substance that produces a flow of tears that temporarily blinds a person; tear gas

lethal agent—a substance that causes death

Lewisite—a blistering agent similar in effect to mustard gas

mustard gas—a blistering agent with an odor like that of mustard or garlic

national technical means of inspection—the process in which nations rely on their own means of verification

nerve agent—a chemical substance that disrupts the enzyme essential to transmitting messages between nerves and muscles

orticant—a chemical agent that creates an itching rash or stinging sensation

pathogen—an agent that causes disease

pharmaceutical—relating to the manufacture and sale of drugs *phosgene*—a lung agent that can lead to death

precursor—a substance from which another product is formed

projectile—a self-propelling missile

proliferation—a rapid increase

ratify—approve

ricin—a deadly toxin made from castor beans

rickettsiae—a group of bacteria that must be grown in living tissue

sanction—a penalty for violating an agreement

sarin—a nerve agent invented by a German scientist in 1938

spore—protective cell with a hard coating that allows bacteria to exist in an inactive state for years

sternutator—a chemical agent that causes sneezing and coughing

synthesize—to combine to form a new product

terrorism—politically motivated violence

Third World—poorer, developing nations

toxic—poisonous

toxin—a poisonous substance made by living organisms or synthetic processes

universality—the application of rules to all countries, rather than a few or even most

vaccine—a preparation of microorganisms that is given for protection against certain diseases

verification—the certainty that each party to an agreement complies with the terms of the agreement

vesicant—see blistering agent

virus—an organism smaller than a bacterium that consists of genetic material surrounded by a protective coat

VX—a nerve agent

weapons of mass destruction (WMD)—nuclear, biological, and chemical weapons

yellow rain—a term used to describe chemical weapons that may have been used in Southeast Asia and Afghanistan beginning in the 1970s

Nonfiction Books

Alibek, Ken. *Biohazard: The Chilling True Story of the Largest Covert Biological Weapons Program in the World, Told from the Inside by the Man Who Ran It.* New York: Random House, 1999.

Cole, Leonard A. *The Eleventh Plague: The Politics of Biological and Chemical Warfare.* New York: W. H. Freeman, 1997.

Landau, Elaine. *Chemical and Biological Warfare.* New York: Lodestar Books, 1991.

Levy, Beth, ed. *Chemical and Biological Warfare.* New York: H.W. Wilson, 1999.

Mangold, Tom. *Plague Wars: The Terrifying Reality of Biological Warfare.* New York: St. Martin's Press, 1999.

Pringle, Laurence. *Chemical and Biological Warfare: The Cruelest Weapons.* rev. ed. Berkeley Heights, N.J.: Enslow Publishers, 2000.

Taylor, C.L., and L.B. Taylor, Jr. *Chemical and Biological Warfare.* rev. ed. New York: Franklin Watts, 1992.

Fiction Books

Cook, Robin. *Vector.* New York: G.P. Putnam & Sons, 1999.

Preston, Richard. *The Cobra Event.* New York: Random House, 1997.

Organizations and Websites

Arms Control Association
1726 M St., N.W., Suite 201
Washington, DC 20036
http://www.armscontrol.org

> The Arms Control Association is a national nonpartisan membership organization dedicated to promoting public understanding of and support for effective arms control policies.

The Center for Security Policy
1920 L St., N.W., Suite 210
Washington, DC 20036
http://www.security-policy.org

> The Center for Security Policy exists as a nonprofit, nonpartisan organization to stimulate and inform the national and international debate about all aspects of security policy, notably those policies bearing on foreign, defense, economic, financial, and technology interests of the United States.

Chemical and Biological Defense
  Information Analysis Center
P.O. Box 196
Gunpowder Branch APG, MD 21010-0196
http://www.cbiac.apgea.army.mil

> The Chemical and Biological Defense Information Analysis Center is a Department of Defense information center.

Federation of American Scientists
307 Massachusetts Ave., N.E.
Washington, DC 20002
http://www.fas.org

> The Federation of American Scientists is engaged in analysis and advocacy on science, technology, and public policy for global security.

Henry L. Stimson Center
11 Dupont Circle, N.W., Ninth Floor
Washington, DC 20036
http://www.stimson.org
> The Henry L. Stimson Center is an independent, nonprofit public policy institute committed to finding and promoting solutions to the security challenges confronting the United States and other nations in the twenty-first century.

U.S. Department of State, Bureau of Arms Control
2201 C St., N.W.
Washington, DC 20520
http://www.acda.gov
> The Bureau of Arms Control in the U.S. Department of State is responsible for international agreements on conventional, chemical/biological, and strategic forces, treaty verification, policy-making, and interagency implementation efforts.

SOURCES

Introduction

Brackett, D.W. *Holy Terror: Armageddon in Tokyo*. New York: Weatherhill, 1996.

Broad, William, Sheryl WuDunn, and Judith Miller. "How Japan Germ Terror Alerted World." *New York Times*, May 26, 1998, pp. A1 and A10.

Cooper, Mary. "Chemical and Biological Weapons." *CQ Researcher* 7, No. 4 (January 31, 1997): 73–96.

Kaplan, David E., and Andrew Marshall. *The Cult at the End of the World*. New York: Crown, 1996.

Nelan, Bruce W. "The Price of Fanaticism." *Time* 145, No. 14 (April 3, 1995): 38–41.

Van Biema, David. "Prophet of Poison." *Time* 145, No. 14 (April 3, 1995): 26–33.

Chapter 1

Marrs, Timothy C., Robert L. Maynard, and Frederick R. Sidell. *Chemical Warfare Agents: Toxicology and Treatment*. Chichester, Eng.: Wiley, 1996.

Norris, John, and Will Fowler. *NBC: Nuclear, Biological and Chemical Warfare on the Modern Battlefield*. London: Brassey's, 1997.

Spiers, Edward M. *Chemical Weaponry: A Continuing Challenge*. New York: St. Martin's Press, 1989.

Utgoff, Victor A. *The Challenge of Chemical Weapons*. New York: St. Martin's Press, 1991.

Wright, Susan, ed. *Preventing a Biological Arms Race*. Cambridge, Mass.: MIT Press, 1990.

Chapter 2

Ali, Jared, Leslie Rodriguez, and Michael Moodie. *Jane's U.S. Chemical-Biological Defense Guidebook*. Alexandria, Va.: Jane's Information Group, 1997.

Buck, George. *Preparing for Terrorism: An Emergency Services Guide*. Albany, N.Y.: Delmar Publishers, 1997.

Committee on R & D Needs for Improving Civilian Medical Response to Chemical and Biological Terrorism Incidents, Health Science Program, Institute of Medicine and Board on Environmental Studies and Toxicology, Commission on Life Sciences, National Research Council. *Chemical and Biological Terrorism: Research and Development to Improve Civilian Medical Response*. Washington, D.C.: National Academy Press, 1999.

Ellis, John W. *Police Analysis and Planning for Chemical, Biological, and Radiological Attacks: Prevention, Defense, and Response*. Springfield, Ill.: Charles C. Thomas Publisher, 1999.

Graham, Bradley. "Local Authorities Train to Handle New Threat." *Washington Post*, January 6, 1998, pp. A1, A6.

U.S. Public Health Service, Office of Emergency Preparedness. *Proceedings of the Seminar on Responding to the Consequences of Chemical and Biological Terrorism*. Washington, D.C.: Government Printing Office, 1996.

Chapter 3

Alibek, Ken. *Biohazard: The Chilling True Story of the Largest Covert Biological Weapons Program in the World, Told from the Inside by the Man Who Ran It*. New York: Random House, 1999.

Cole, Leonard A. *Clouds of Secrecy: The Army's Germ Warfare Tests over Populated Areas*. Totawa, N.J: Rowman & Littlefield, 1988.

_____. *The Eleventh Plague: The Politics of Biological and Chemical Warfare*. New York: W.H. Freeman, 1997.

Haber, L.H. *The Poisonous Cloud: Chemical Warfare in the First World War*. Oxford, Eng.: Clarendon Press, 1986.

Pelletiere, Steven C., and Douglas V. Johnson, II. *Lessons Learned: The Iran-Iraq War*. Carlisle Barracks, Pa.: Strategic Studies Institute, U.S. Army War College, 1991.

Piller, Charles, and Keith Yamamoto. *Gene Wars: Military Control Over the New Genetic Technologies*. New York: Birch Tree Books, William Morrow, 1988.

Stockholm International Peace Research Institute (SIPRI). *The Problem of Chemical and Biological Warfare: Vol. I: The Rise of CB Weapons*. Stockholm: Almqvist & Wiksell and New York: Humanities Press, 1971.

Tucker, Jonathan B. "The Biological Weapons Threat." *Current History* 96, No. 609 (April 1997): 167–172.

Chapter 4

Bailey, Kathleen C. *Doomsday Weapons in the Hands of the Many: The New Arms Control Challenge of the 90s*. Urbana: University of Illinois Press, 1991.

Dando, Malcolm. *Biological Warfare in the 21st Century: Biotechnology and the Proliferation of Biological Weapons*. London and New York: Brassey's (UK), 1994.

Ekeus, Ambassador Rolf. "Leaving Behind the UNSCOM Legacy in Iraq." *Arms Control Today*. 27, No. 4 (June/July 1997): 3–6.

Forsberg, Randall, William Driscoll, Gregory Webb, and Jonathan Dean. *Nonproliferation Primer: Preventing the Spread of Nuclear, Chemical, and Biological Weapons*. Cambridge, Mass.: MIT Press, 1995.

Gellman, Barton. "The Hunt for Iraq's Forbidden Weapons: Game of Hide and Seek." *Washington Post*, October 11, 1998, pp. A1 and A42–A43.

_____. "The Hunt for Iraq's Forbidden Weapons: Arms Inspectors Shake the Tree." *Washington Post*, October 12, 1998, pp. A1 and A16–A17.

Haselkorn, Avigdor. *The Continuing Storm: Iraq, Poisonous Weapons and Deterrence.* New Haven, Conn.: Yale University Press, 1999.

Ritter, Scott. *Endgame: Solving the Iraq Problem—Once and for All.* New York: Simon and Schuster, 1999.

Roberts, Brad, ed. *Biological Weapons: Weapons of the Future?* Washington, D.C.: Center for Strategic and International Studies, 1993.

Schneider, Barry R. *Future War and Counterproliferation: U.S. Military Responses to NBC Proliferation Threats.* Westport, Conn.: Praeger, 1999.

Smith, R. Jeffrey. "Iraq's Drive for a Biological Arsenal." *Washington Post*, November 21, 1997, pp. A1, A48–A49.

Spiers, Edward M. *Chemical and Biological Weapons: A Study of Proliferation.* New York: St. Martin's Press, 1994.

U.S. Congress. Office of Technology Assessment. *Proliferation of Weapons of Mass Destruction: Assessing the Risks.* Washington, D.C.: U.S. Government Printing Office, August 1993.

Chapter 5

Douglass, Joseph D., Jr., and Neil C. Livingstone. *America the Vulnerable: The Threat of Chemical and Biological Warfare.* Lexington, Mass.: Lexington Books, 1987.

Falkenrath, Richard A., Robert D. Newman, and Bradley A. Thayer. *America's Achilles Heel: Nuclear, Biological, and Chemical Terrorism and Covert Attack.* Cambridge, Mass.: MIT Press, 1998.

Jenkins, Brian. "Playing on Fears of a New World Disorder." *Los Angeles Times*, March 24, 1995, p. B7.

Laqueur, Walter. "Postmodern Terrorism." *Foreign Affairs* 75, No. 5 (September/October 1996): 24–36.

Simon, Jeffrey D. *Terrorists and the Potential Use of Biological Weapons*. Santa Monica, Calif. Rand, 1989.

Stern, Jessica. *The Ultimate Terrorists*. Cambridge, Mass: Harvard University Press, 1999.

Tucker, Jonathan B., and Amy Sands. "An Unlikely Threat." *Bulletin of the Atomic Scientists* 55, No. 4 (July/August 1999): 46–52.

Chapter 6

Adams, Valerie. *Chemical Warfare, Chemical Disarmament*. Bloomington: Indiana University Press, 1990.

Broad, William J., and Judith Miller. "Government Report Says 3 Nations Hold Stocks of Smallpox." *New York Times*, June 13, 1999, pp. 1 and 12.

Crone, Hugh D. *Banning Chemical Weapons*. New York: Cambridge University Press, 1992.

Kessler, J. Christian. *Verifying Nonproliferation Treaties: Obligation, Process, and Sovereignty*. Washington, D.C.: National Defense University Press, 1995.

Moon, John Ellis Van Courtland. "Controlling Chemical and Biological Weapons Through World War II." In *Encyclopedia of Arms Control and Disarmament,* edited by Richard D. Burns, vol. 2, pp. 657–674. New York: Charles Scribner's Sons, 1993.

Morel, Benoit, and Kyle Olson, eds. *Shadows and Substance: The Chemical Weapons Convention*. Boulder, Colo.: Westview Press, 1993.

Price, Richard M. *The Chemical Weapons Taboo*. Ithaca, N.Y.: Cornell University Press, 1997.

Smithson, Amy. "Playing Politics with the Chemical Weapons Convention." *Current History* 96, No. 609 (April 1997): 162–166.

Stockholm International Peace Research Institute. *The Problem of Chemical and Biological Warfare: Vol. IV: CB*

Disarmament Negotiations, 1920–1970. Stockholm: Almqvist & Wiksell, and New York: Humanities Press, 1971.

Chapter 7

Cordesman, Anthony H. *Iraq and the War of Sanctions: Conventional Threats and Weapons of Mass Destruction.* Westport, Conn.: Praeger, 1999.

Haar, Barend ter. *The Future of Biological Weapons.* New York: Praeger, 1991.

U.S. Cong., Senate. *Global Proliferation of Weapons of Mass Destruction.* Hearings before the Permanent Subcommittee on Investigations of the Committee on Governmental Affairs. 104th Cong. 1st Sess., 1995–1996.

INDEX

Herbert M. Levine is a political scientist and writer. He taught political science for 20 years at the University of Southwestern Louisiana, where he won two teaching awards. He left a teaching career as a professor of political science to persue his writing interests in the Washington, D.C., metropolitan area.

He is the author most recently of four books for young adults in the American Issues Debated series. These books deal with controversial issues—gun control, animal rights, the drug problem, and immigration—in a debate format. He has written other books, including college textbooks in political science, a memoir of the highest ranked woman in the U.S. Navy, and an evaluation of the animal rights' movement, as well as articles that have appeared in academic journals, popular magazines, newspapers, and reference books. In addition, he is a consultant in a publishing program for students.

He has a Ph.D. in political science from Columbia University and currently lives in Chevy Chase, Maryland.

PROPERTY OF
SOUTH KNOX SCHOOLS